Praise for *The Woman's Book of Joy*

"This book is full of bite-sized treasures. Grab a cup of tea and let the affirmations sink in and nurture your soul. A comforting and life-affirming read."

—Laura Berman Fortgang, author of *The Little Book on Meaning* and *Living Your Best Life*

"Eileen Campbell has written a book of poignant truths that will help you remember who you really are and what you really want. Each chapter of this book is a powerful meditation that calms your nervous system and helps you reconnect with your grace."

—Tama Kieves, bestselling author of *This Time I Dance! Creating the Work You Love*, *Inspired & Unstoppable*, and *A Year Without Fear: 365 Days of Magnificence* www.TamaKieves.com

"*The Woman's Book of Joy* addresses ways our inherent capacity for joy can be dampened or even deep-sixed for a while. Thankfully, the book's helpful suggestions and affirmations give readers many guidelines for inviting joy to reign in their hearts again. I especially appreciate the author's reminders to be gentle with ourselves as we heal and move once again toward joy."

—Sue Patton Thoele, author of *The Courage to Be Yourself* and *The Woman's Book of Confidence*

The
Woman's Book
of Joy

The
Woman's Book
of Joy

Listen to Your Heart,
Live with Gratitude, and Find Your Bliss

Eileen Campbell

Conari Press

This edition first published in 2016 by Conari Press, an imprint of
Red Wheel/Weiser, LLC
With offices at:
65 Parker Street, Suite 7
Newburyport, MA 01950
www.redwheelweiser.com

ISBN: 978-1-57324-670-5

Library of Congress Cataloging-in-Publication Data available upon
request.

Cover design by Jim Warner
Cover art: Salvation (oil on panel), Campbell, Rebecca
    Private Collection/Courtesy of Jonathan Cooper, Park Walk Gallery,
    London, Bridgeman Images
Interior by Deborah Dutton
Typeset in Weiss text and Mrs Eaves display

Printed in Canada
MAR
10 9 8 7 6 5 4 3 2 1

Contents

II. Developing awareness   31

III. Letting go of negative emotions   59

IV. Cultivating optimism   91

V. Believing in our dreams 117

VI. Practicing kindness 141

VII. Trusting life's process   169

x. Finding our unique purpose 239

Introduction

Deep within us exists a vast reservoir of pure joy that we have all on occasion probably experienced, but that we're generally disconnected from, so that it's like we're tuned to the wrong station when trying to listen to a specific program on the radio.

We long for a harmony of life, work, and relationships, but we all inevitably have to grapple with difficult issues of one kind or another and often feel fragmented because of the contradictory tensions and distractions in our lives. In times of difficulty when fear or despair seem to overwhelm us, or when we feel inadequate, this reservoir is exactly what we need to access, for it can help us through our troubles.

We need to remind ourselves that it is always available to us no matter what is happening. When we're crippled by doubt and anxiety, we don't always think of turning inward for help. Loving arms, gentle words, and patient listening by family or friends can help enormously when they are available, but all too often we find ourselves alone in our crises. It's then that the inspiring words of others can help point us in the right direction—to look within ourselves.

Many years ago, when I was consumed with pain and sadness, I began to keep a book of inspirational quotes. Every time I came across some uplifting words or something that resonated with how I was feeling, I jotted them down. I consequently found that whenever I felt low, just ten minutes or so of reading inspiring words helped me in my journey of understanding, and made me more able to bear what I was experiencing. I realized that through the process of healing, I was learning more about myself. I developed greater strength to weather future storms, and I also began to feel a sense of expansion, connecting with a power greater than myself. As a result I experienced feelings of real joy.

What I offer here comes from my own experience and what I've learned from others who have opened my eyes and inspired me. I hope to encourage women everywhere to feel that there is a way out of the despair they sometimes feel. We all have the capacity to heal ourselves. Using *The Woman's Book of Joy*, by reading and reflecting on a section and adopting an affirmation and working with it, we can begin the process of healing.

Although we can't always control what happens to us in life, we can choose to seek a different way of looking at things, and however difficult the situation, we find that things begin to change. Over time we come to realize just how precious this Source of joy is that we have deep within us. Accessing it, we can appreciate how strong we really are and can live more authentically, in touch with our true selves. We naturally become more loving because we feel more whole and are in tune with our purpose. We can be more confident about a future that is fulfilling and exciting, and find ourselves radiating joy to all those around us.

May your life be full of joy whatever the challenges you face!

The
Woman's Book
of Joy

Chapter I

Finding courage

*To have courage for whatever comes in life—
everything lies in that.*
SAINT TERESA OF AVILA

It takes courage to be fully human, to wake up to life's possibilities, and to grow and mature. When we take a step from the known to the unknown, whether it's our first day at college, embarking on our career, or starting a new relationship, there's always a degree of trepidation amidst the excitement. It takes even greater courage to deal with the challenges that are part of everyone's life sooner or later.

Fear is something we all feel, and unexamined fear can cause a great deal of our suffering. Life rarely turns out the way we want it to, and we have to find the courage to deal with the disappointments, losses, or tragedies that we encounter, and not be held back by our fears. We may try to protect ourselves from suffering by building defenses, but we have to learn to face the painful feelings instead of trying to avoid them. When we do, we find that pain has a useful function—it ultimately enables us to have a greater capacity for joy. In his poem "The Guest House," Rumi, the thirteenth-century Persian Sufi poet, points out how we can welcome in the painful feelings because there is much that we can learn from them:

> Welcome and entertain them all!
> Even if they're a crowd of sorrows,
> who violently sweep your house
> empty of its furniture,
> still treat each guest honorably.
> He may be clearing you out
> for some new delight.
> The dark thought, the shame, the malice,
> meet them at the door laughing,
> and invite them in.

We need to be open to everything in life, and yet being open is a risk. We may be fearful of taking risks because of our past unhappy experiences, but risk must be taken, for without it we cannot learn or grow. When we dare to live our lives with courage, we live more spontaneously. We are no longer afraid to be ourselves and find our own way through the complexities of life. When we face up to what has to be done, we surprise ourselves by finding that we are far stronger than we could ever have imagined. We survive and live to tell the tale. We've learned by trying, failing, and trying again. We're no longer afraid to reveal ourselves with all our imperfections and weaknesses, and we don't try to pretend we're someone we're not in order to fit in or please someone else. We can be our authentic selves, who we truly are.

When we come to realize that everything changes anyway, we're no longer afraid of what may lie ahead. As we age and have to cope with the gradual loss of our energy and health, and all that accompanies old age, the greatest challenge still lies ahead. Why should dying be any different from the rest of our life experiences? By then we will have coped with much that has been difficult and painful, and our lives are richer by far with accumulated wisdom. Death will be no different if we face it courageously and with equanimity. By then we know full well that life is a spiritual journey and that every experience is for our growth and learning.

I. Recognizing our fears

We all experience fear in our lives, and there's nothing wrong with that. It's a valid response to uncertainty and danger. Who wouldn't feel afraid in the face of war, a deadly disease, or extreme weather conditions? More often though, we're afraid of losing our job, our home, our partner, or our children; we may fear getting sick or growing old; we almost certainly fear dying.

There are other more subtle fears that we're largely unaware of and are at the root of many of our habits. They can have a detrimental effect on the quality of our lives and our capacity for joy. They are devious and pop up when we least expect them. We can find ourselves fearing being inadequate, or not good enough; we can be fearful of speaking out, or initiating change, preferring instead to stay with what we're familiar with rather than taking a chance. Fear can run riot, permeating our thoughts and increasing in intensity. A chance remark, a misunderstood email, a lover not being where they told us they were—we imagine the worst-case scenario, and our insecurity feeds the tangle of spiraling thoughts until we feel utterly miserable and our stomach is knotted.

Such fears have their roots in the past. They arise from the subconscious patterns established in childhood. When our behavior as kids was met with disapproval, ridicule, punishment, or, sadly, in some cases violence, primarily from our parents, siblings, or teachers, we reacted in ways that resulted in low self-esteem, anxiety, guilt, or depression. Our deep-seated fears of not getting what we need, or being abandoned, or feeling vulnerable get triggered when things don't work out in our lives. We may try to protect ourselves by putting on a front of perfectionism or cynicism, or we may try to avoid the pain of these feelings by an activity that helps numb the fears, like drinking more than we should, working incessantly, or shopping compulsively.

We have to recognize these feelings for what they are since they are still festering inside us. We can do this by trying to be present and staying with the fears rather than wanting them to go away. We need to be gentle with ourselves and give ourselves the love we are afraid we won't get. When we make a decision to work at this, things gradually begin to shift, and our fears subside.

I know that fear is just a feeling.

I am secure.

I have all the love I need.

2. Taking risks

"Risk! Risk anything! . . . Do the hardest thing on earth for you. Act for yourself. Face the truth," advised the writer Katherine Mansfield.

We tend to stay with the known, the familiar, rather than risk the unknown. Taking risks is scary— we might fail, be rejected, experience loss or disappointment, and nothing might turn out as we hope. Sometimes, though, the unknown may be less risky than staying put, such as staying in an abusive relationship that puts one's life in danger. Generally we cannot protect ourselves by not taking risks, and we're certainly unlikely to have rich and rewarding life experiences. We definitely can't grow and mature. If we don't take risks life is not being lived, and we may experience fear, loneliness, and lack of fulfillment. "The day came," wrote the author Anaïs Nin, "when the risk to remain tight in a bud was more painful than the risk it took to blossom."

Taking risks means being open to life's experiences, being curious about what might be if we were to do something different, break away, or speak out and challenge. When we find the courage to take that risk we feel energized and alive—we're no longer trapped in some half-dead existence. We're opening ourselves to the possibility of more joy in our lives.

Being curious about life's unfolding and taking risks isn't necessarily reserved for the young either. It's just as relevant as we age. Too often a bad experience in the past can prevent us from taking a risk in the future, and we "play it safe," which is never really "safe." When we fail to take risks, we limit the possibility of new and exciting experiences in our lives. Instead we may well become stunted as human beings, afraid of change, and less resilient in the face of misfortune. When a relationship comes to an end, we may feel nervous about embarking on another; after a car accident it's not easy to get back behind the wheel; or we may stay in a job in which we're unhappy simply because we made a change once before that didn't work out.

We don't need to be limited by what happened in the past. We can choose new possibilities; though taking risks involves effort and practice. Just as with exercising, we become better at it the more we do it, until it becomes a habit. And once risk-taking becomes a habit, and we're prepared to live with the consequences, whatever they may be, knowing that we can get up and keep on trying, then life itself becomes "a daring adventure," to use Helen Keller's phrase. She certainly had a courageous life in spite of being deaf and blind. When we take risks we have a greater opportunity for more joy in our lives.

I am receptive to life's experiences.
I am not afraid to take risks.

3. Daring to be ourselves

It's not easy being ourselves—it takes courage to let people see who we really are. Do we know who we are really, and what we truly want out of life? How can we find the joy deep within us?

We have created a concept of ourselves, our ego, or self-image. This has been built up since our childhood. From birth to around age six we acquired certain perceptions from our parents, siblings, and other relatives, and we learned what behaviors were acceptable to them. Likewise, as we grew up we were influenced by teachers at school, friends, and society in general. We create stories about who we are, defining ourselves by our family and friends, by our education, by our job, and by our interests.

All too often we play a role, yet underneath we're a bundle of fears, largely because we were never given a sense of unconditional approval. We see ourselves as separate from everything and everyone, which leaves us with a sense of being incomplete. Living in a society that is competitive, materialistic, and superficial, and that does not promote cooperative and compassionate values, we do our best to fit in. As Henry David Thoreau pointed out in *Walden*, "The mass of men live lives of quiet desperation."

Sometimes, however, a crossroads is reached—we sense a need to live differently. The authentic self is calling us and we need to listen to the whispers coming from our hearts. We need to find out who we truly are, and what we really want and need for our growth.

Sometimes we feel guilty when we focus on our own needs and do something for ourselves, but it is vital that we do and don't ignore the yearnings for something better. We need to turn inward to find answers. We have to give ourselves the space to explore our feelings and thoughts, and question our assumptions. Only then can we become clearer about what is important to us and reorganize our priorities so that they are meaningful to us and give purpose to the days, weeks, and years. We need to attend to those priorities, carving out time for them, so that we can get in touch with who we truly are, and find what will make our hearts sing.

The Indian teacher Sri Sathya Sai Baba taught that we're actually three people and suggested we try to make them one. "There is the one you think you are, the one others think you are, and the one you really are." If we can make them one, joy, peace, and bliss will be the result.

I am not afraid to discover who I am.
I dare to be myself.
I am willing to live differently.

4. Facing emotional pain

We cannot avoid emotional pain in life, and it's through our experience of it that we come to understand what it means to be human. Kahlil Gibran, the Lebanese poet and mystic, wrote movingly in his popular classic *The Prophet*:

Your pain is the breaking of the shell
that encloses your understanding.
Even as the stone of the fruit must break,
that its heart may stand in the sun,
so must you know pain . . .

Through the experience of pain, we learn humility and compassion, and in dealing with it we become stronger and more resilient.

When we feel sad, lonely, or afraid, we usually try to distract ourselves to avoid confronting and feeling overwhelmed by the pain. We keep busy, we eat and drink too much, we shop, we watch TV, we gamble—we do these things compulsively and to excess so that we blot out the discomfort we're feeling. There are consequences to all this, however, which exacerbate the situation. The distractions only work for a while, and the pain is still there, gnawing away. Feeling miserable and alone in our suffering increases the risk of everything from depression to dementia. Our immune systems begin to function poorly, and we are more likely to go on to suffer heart attacks.

We often don't get what we feel we want in life, and we sometimes lose what we have. Whilst emotional pain is inevitable, suffering isn't. We can choose not to suffer. We can choose to face our pain, accept what has happened to cause the hurt, and then let go of it. We can stop going over and over the story we've told ourselves. "As long as you make an identity for yourself out of pain, you cannot be free of it," writes the spiritual teacher Eckhart Tolle.

We can become more aware of how our mind keeps us trapped in pain by its continual replaying of the old tapes. We need to let go of this and move on. One of the most effective ways of doing this is to relax the body and focus on our breathing, just observing the flow of the breath in and out of our nostrils. When we do this we find that the breath slows and we begin to feel more at ease. We can observe our thoughts and see them for what they are—just thoughts. Gradually we begin to feel that things are not so bad, we see things differently and realize that we can let go of the pain.

I choose to accept what has happened.
I can change the story I tell myself.
I let go of the pain.

5. Finding a path back to life after tragedy

The whole of life is a series of beginnings and endings, a succession of mini-deaths, that we have to learn to take in our stride, whether it's the loss of youth and our looks, or a long-standing relationship that has finished, or retirement after a lifetime of work. Sometimes, however, real tragedy strikes and our world falls apart. The sudden death of one's partner or the loss of a child in a terrible accident, a fire destroying our home, an unexpected joblessness; when such events come in a flash, out of the blue, they leave a trail of grief and devastation. As we move through a range of emotions—rage, despair, and hopelessness—they may seem impossible to deal with. When our hearts are aching we somehow have to find the inner resources to carry on. We have to try to stay with what we're feeling, rather than attempting to escape the pain by whatever means we can.

No matter what we have lost in life, we have the power to begin again. The healing of our wounds and the rebuilding of our lives may take a long time. We need to try and see things differently, shifting our perspective from what we have lost to focusing on what we still have in our lives. There is no place for despair because life is too precious to waste in cutting ourselves off. We need to accept that the world is full of chaos and that life is unpredictable, that we got caught in the eye of the storm, but that there can also be calm afterwards.

We all have the capacity to experience joy once again. When we stop struggling, when we are gentle with ourselves, and take time to look within, we come to know ourselves better. We realize that life does go on and that it is indeed worth living.

Many have succeeded in making something out of their suffering. Brooke Ellison became a quadriplegic after being struck by a car. This hasn't stopped her from obtaining a master's degree in public policy from Harvard University, completing a PhD, and running for the New York State Senate—with the help and loving support of her mother. She has traveled the US as a motivational speaker, has been involved in research in the stem cell field, and is a faculty member at Stony Brook University.

Victoria Mulligan was a happily married woman with four children, a house in London and a holiday home in Cornwall. Only with hindsight did she come to see how lucky she and her family were. One summer's day, however, her family's life changed forever when a tragic boating accident took away her husband, her daughter, as well as her own left, lower leg. A year later, Victoria learned to walk with a prosthetic leg. She realizes now that through this tragic experience she knows much more about herself. As survivors, she and the three children have accepted that they have to live their lives not only for themselves, but also for her husband and the daughter who are no longer here.

I have all the inner resources I need.

I have the power to begin again.

I know that life is worth living whatever my circumstances.

6. Embracing change and opening to possibilities

The rate of change in our world seems to be increasing exponentially, and no sooner do we get accustomed to one set of changes then there are yet more. We can become anxious because we never know what's going to happen next, and we tend to prefer to stay with what we know and feel relatively comfortable with, staying perhaps longer in relationships, jobs, and situations than might be good for our development. We try to control things so that we can be sure (or so we think!) that we know what's going to happen. Control can work up to a point; it's good to be organized if we're planning a holiday—we book the flight, we pack the clothes we think we will need, we check we have our passports, travel documents, etc., but we cannot control the airport delays, the loss of our luggage, the hotel burning down, or, indeed, the weather being unseasonably inclement.

There are too many unexpected events in life. It's impossible to prevent them, and we cannot protect ourselves and have everything just as we would like. We have to be courageous in the face of change, and we need to be open and flexible. The reason we get upset when things change is because we're unable to be flexible. We want things to be the way we planned them. If, however, we can be open to the reality that everything changes all the time, and if we can learn to adapt, we realize that there is no reason to suffer.

It requires courage, of course, to allow whatever is happening to unfold. We have to assess the situation honestly and make whatever adjustments we can. We need to soften and be curious, rather than battling on, refusing to let go of our habits and beliefs. It requires practice, but the more we try to be flexible and not push to achieve the outcome we want for ourselves, the less we're inclined to suffer. We need to let go of old patterns of thinking, for embracing change is the only way of ensuring our lives are filled with joy. When we accept responsibility for where we are, we are empowered to change things, and we learn to make new and better choices.

If we look back on our lives, we usually find that something that was really distressing at the time turned out to be something that benefited us. The relationship that ended with heartbreak freed us ultimately to have a very different kind of relationship, bringing us great happiness. Or the unemployment that caused us so much anger and upset led to us starting our own business, which was far more fulfilling.

Being open to possibilities is vital on our journey through life, because when we're open, new and different opportunities present themselves. We see things we may have missed before, and we begin to appreciate all the good things about life and people around us. We feel connected rather than isolated and anxious.

I am willing to be more flexible.
I can let go of old patterns of thinking.
I am making new and better choices.

Finding courage

7. Seeing crisis as an opportunity for growth

How often has life appeared to be running reasonably smoothly, apart from the occasional blip, when suddenly we're plunged into mayhem? We didn't heed the warning signs, we missed something staring us in the face because we were too busy and not paying attention, we plowed on thinking everything was okay, only to pay the price when our world came crashing down around our ears.

Often such a crisis is a wake-up call. Only by stopping, facing the difficult circumstances, and taking stock and reassessing our lives can we deal with the crisis in a meaningful way. In the process we are presented with an opportunity to grow as human beings.

After thirty-five years of marriage, Jill discovered that her husband was having an affair that had become more important to her husband than their marriage. She was completely devastated—angry, distraught, unable to sleep or eat. The pain was unbearable initially. Jill had married whilst very young and still living at home with her parents. She had never been on her own for any length of time, so her husband's departure was a completely new experience for her, her sons having more or less grown up and left home. It took some time, but gradually as the weeks turned to months, and then years, she realized that the new life that was emerging was far richer than her previous existence. She made new friends, took up new interests, traveled and saw something of the world, but above all, for the first time in her life, she began to know who she really was and what it was that she wanted out of life.

We may not always want to embrace the misfortunes in our lives, but if we can come to see them as opportunities to live our lives differently, to make different choices, and have more meaningful experiences, then life blossoms and we grow in wisdom.

I'm reminded of the genesis of a pearl. A particle of sand or a tiny piece of seaweed gets into the body of an oyster. It's an irritant and painful, so the oyster attempts to expel it, but cannot. Instead, the oyster tries another way—she secretes layer upon layer of nacre around the obstacle, so that it becomes a lustrous pearl.

Like the oyster, we too can choose to resist or accept the obstacles in our lives. Over time each painful experience can be transformed into something meaningful. When we are open to the experience, however difficult it is, and endeavor to integrate it into our lives, a beautiful transformation occurs. Instead of hardening our hearts and closing up, if we soften and yield, we enable joy to well up from inside us.

🦋

I choose to accept the challenges confronting me.
I am growing as a human being.
I am open to the possibility of something new.

8. Celebrating aging rather than fearing it

Life becomes more precious to us as we age. We experience time speeding up as we begin to slow down, and there is a growing understanding that we will not live forever.

We look in the mirror and see a face and body we barely recognize. We creak and shuffle when we get up in the morning, but we know deep down that we are more than our aging faces and bodies. By this point in our lives we have a wealth of memories, life experiences, and knowledge. We suffer less from fear and can speak our mind, and we're more comfortable in our own skin. We can do what we want when we want and perhaps never had the time to do before.

It's never too late to take up a new interest, or hobby, or a course of study. We can still grow and live fulfilling lives. We may not have had the opportunity to do something we wanted to do when we were younger, or we may have been discouraged from attempting something.

As a young girl, I remember being told by the art teacher at my school that I had no talent for painting. In more recent years, knowing of my love of gardening and flowers, a friend who is an accomplished botanical artist suggested that I try one of her workshops. I decided to give it a go—I felt I had nothing to lose and it was worth taking the risk. After three days of working diligently, I could scarcely hold back the tears when I saw the results of my attention, my desire to paint, and most importantly my friend's encouragement. For years I had believed that this was not something I could do, and although hardly a masterpiece, this, my first attempt, felt like a miracle. Since then I have often sat down to draw or paint, and am thrilled to think this new interest is something I can enjoy.

With our extended lifespan, there is no reason for us to be less passionate about living, and sharing our experience with others, passing on our wisdom and understanding. We can also turn inward and reflect on our lives as we become less able to be active. The human spirit can grow stronger and we can love and feel loved for ourselves and who we are.

I choose to keep on taking risks.
I am passionate about life and learning.
I trust the future.

9. Dealing with illness and recovery

Serious illness, whether in ourselves or those we love, requires courage if we're to deal with it when it occurs, as well as the implications for our lives afterwards. Illness shatters the illusion that we're in control of our bodies, while the process of recovery means that life does not continue as before. We are forced to reexamine our lives, reassess our lifestyle, and make changes. On the one hand we replace bad habits that may have contributed to our ill-health, whether it's addressing our diet and exercising more, or eliminating stress and finding more time for relaxation. We also may dig deeper to find out who we are in the process of recovering.

My only experience of serious illness was to contract cerebral malaria and not have it diagnosed quickly enough, which meant that I ended up hospitalized for ten days. The month-long recovery period that followed caused me to reevaluate my life. I decided to shed some of my work responsibilities as a way of eliminating some of the stress in my life, which had probably contributed to weakening my immune system. I also decided to create more space to pursue my creative interests, which I knew would enrich my life.

The writer, Nandini Murati, writes of illness that it's, "a journey within that helps us seek, discover, and reclaim ourselves." Illness may disrupt our lives, but at the same time it can also bring transformative benefits. When we understand how little time we have on this earth, it does raise questions for us about the meaning and purpose of life. It changes the way we view the world and as a result we live more fully and deeply. We can achieve far more than we ever imagined possible when we were in full health, and joy is able to manifest to a greater extent in our lives.

Hilary Lister is someone who has triumphed over a cruel illness to be an inspiration for us all. When she was eleven years old early symptoms emerged of a progressive neurological disease: reflex sympathetic dystrophy. In spite of gradually losing the use of her legs and then arms, she completed a degree in biochemistry at Jesus College, Oxford, and most of her PhD at the University of Kent (she was subsequently awarded an honorary doctorate). Having reached the point of wondering if life was worth living, a friend introduced her to sailing in 2003, which she says gave her life "new meaning and purpose." In 2005 she was the first quadriplegic to sail single-handedly across the English Channel. In 2007 she sailed around the Isle of Wight. In 2009 she was the first paralyzed woman to sail solo around Great Britain, and to sail 1,500 kilometers across the Arabian Sea from Mumbai to Muscat. She now dreams of sailing across the Atlantic. Hilary has now won numerous awards including the Woman of Achievement Award and the *Sunday Times* Sportswoman of the Year. This amazing woman, in spite of lack of movement and debilitating pain, has demonstrated such incredible courage and shows us that illness need not hold us back. We can all achieve miracles in spite of illness if we are courageous.

I am prepared to dig deeper to find out who I am.
I have the courage to live more fully and deeply.
I know that I can achieve miracles.

10. Transforming our perception of dying

None of us want to think too much about dying, and yet it's not a bad idea to be at least a little prepared for death in the midst of life, for we never know when it will come. Death is the one inevitability that none of us is likely to be well prepared for. We no longer sew samplers as women did in the seventeenth and eighteenth centuries to remind them what was to come. We now all expect to die in old age rather than be struck down when we're young, but death's schedule is not of our choosing. There's an old Mexican refrain:

> Get used to dying
> before death arrives,
> for the dead can only live
> and the living can only die.

The Mexicans celebrate the Day of the Dead, which developed from ancient traditions among the pre-Columbian cultures; Brazilians visit cemeteries and churches; the Spanish have parades; in France and some other European countries graves of loved ones are visited on All Souls' Day; in some African cultures ancestors' graves are visited; and in China and Japan ancestors are venerated.

In our culture we tend to fear death, "the unknown region" of the poet Walt Whitman, and we are not taught about death or how to die. Death tends to take place at a distance, and we avoid the subject and feel uncomfortable discussing it. Underlying this evasion is fear of change. We think of death as the end, but all the great spiritual traditions of the world have told us it isn't so. Since everything in nature dies and reemerges in some new form, why should it be any different for us? If we can only shift our perspective, we can find the courage to face death.

Philip Kapleau, the influential Zen Buddhist teacher, has written: "Consider a burning candle: its life is also its death; death and life constantly interact. Just as one cannot experience true joy without having suffered great pain, so life is impossible without death, for they are a single process. Death is life in another form."

We have to find the courage too to deal with the death of those we love. None of us wants a miserable and lingering death for our loved ones. We are all now tending to live longer, but perhaps, as the *New York Times* blogger and author Jane Gross put it, "We live too long and die too slowly." Most people now die in hospitals rather than at home, although palliative care in hospices is increasing, allowing the dying to accept death whilst at the same time being helped with pain relief and anxiety.

I watched my eighty-four-year-old mother struggling with death, after several years of poor health. Although at first she experienced anger, bitterness, and wanting things to be as they had been before, gradually she accepted what was happening. At the time of her passing, she knew she was loved and that she would be at peace at last. It was a time rich with meaning for both of us. I appreciated her for what she had given me over the course of her life, and she lives on, not just in my memory, but in the very person I have become because of her. Her courage to live and raise two girls after the tragically early death of my father remains an inspiration to me.

I am not afraid of change.

I accept that death is part of life.

I am willing to believe that death is not the end.

11. Daring to embark on the spiritual journey

For the most part, we live our lives unconsciously, seeing only what we're conditioned to see. We're caught up in the hurly-burly of a world that is governed by Newtonian and Darwinian cause and effect assumptions, resulting in a culture of competitive individualism. The winner-takes-all approach to life actually goes against the grain. Deep down we know something isn't right about the way we all live, for our fundamental need is one of connection and wholeness, not separation.

Every so often we get a wake-up call in the form of some event that leaves us devastated and wondering what life is all about. Like Dante's hero in *The Divine Comedy*, we suddenly find ourselves lost:

> In the middle of the journey of our life
> I found myself in a dark wood
> For the straight path had been lost.

Dante's hero undertakes a difficult and harrowing journey as a result, but eventually comes back to his life's path. This "road less traveled" is a journey we all ultimately take, whether we realize it or not. The journey is called by many names—the Way, the

Spiritual Path, the Quest—but essentially it's a journey of awakening, and it is a spiritual journey.

The exploration often takes place outside of religious institutions, yet all the world's great religious traditions offer teaching and guidance for this journey of growth. Practices like prayer, meditation, chanting, and ritual all help us to become more self-aware. As we come to know who we truly are and live our lives with that sense of connection to the whole, we grow wiser, stronger, and more resilient. If we are courageous enough to embark on the spiritual journey, joy becomes ever more available to us.

I have the courage to embark on the spiritual journey.
I am becoming wiser, stronger, and more resilient.

Chapter II

Developing
awareness

Don't go outside your house to see the flowers.
My friend, don't bother with that excursion.
Inside your body there are flowers.
One flower has a thousand petals.
That will do for a place to sit.
Sitting there you will have a glimpse of beauty
Inside the body and out of it,
Before gardens and after gardens.

KABIR

If we are to live authentically and radiantly, accessing the joy that is our birthright, then developing awareness is vital, and to do that we have to turn inward. However, training our awareness requires commitment, patience, and discipline.

We begin by pausing, slowing down, and becoming intimate with ourselves. We tend to live our lives on autopilot, but once we schedule time to be alone and silent, we can pay attention to what is going on with us. Facing ourselves is not always comfortable, but as we watch and listen, we become more conscious of the mind's unrelenting chatter. We can choose to control our minds through practicing mindfulness and meditation, and the more we do this on a daily basis, the more we begin to feel peaceful. The experience of joy is within our reach.

Mindfulness and meditation produce changes inside our brains. The new science of brain imaging shows how critical networks in the brain become activated. The parts of the brain associated with positive emotions like happiness and compassion become more active as we meditate regularly. So it's not just a question of feeling peaceful whilst practicing as the benefits carry on beyond. It seems we can literally rebuild the brain's grey matter and increase our wellbeing and the quality of our lives.

We may choose to spend our quiet time in nature. Again, there is a lot of evidence that spending time in a garden, park, or in the wilderness is hugely beneficial, a kind of "eco-therapy" that helps us feel connected to the world around us and the life force that flows through it. In the nineteenth century, the transcendentalist writer, Henry David Thoreau, chose to retreat to Walden Pond for over two years: "I went to the woods because I wished to live deliberately, to front only the essential facts of life, and see if I could not learn what it had to teach, and not, when I came to die, discover that I had not lived." The twentieth-century writer, Anne Morrow Lindbergh, retreated to a cottage on the beach in Florida to find out how she could be at peace. In her beautiful *A Gift from the Sea*, she shares her experiences of letting the beach teach her simplicity, solitude, and freedom to grow.

We can also create our own space to retreat to, whether a room of our own, or the corner of a room or office, where we can have some simple reminder of our need to pause and reflect, or to practice even a few minutes of meditation.

Once we become committed to this journey inward, we begin to know ourselves better. Our perception changes and we begin to understand that things are not as we thought they were, but rather a reflection of our own state of mind. We become more in tune with the intuition we all possess, whether we're aware of it or not. We also become more sensitive in our dealings with others, so that our relationships become more harmonious.

Developing awareness

1. Slowing down and creating space for ourselves

Speed has assumed god-like proportions in our age of acceleration. From the moment we wake up in the morning we're rushing. There seem to be so many tasks to squeeze into the day, whether we're single or part of a boisterous family, and the to-do list never seems to grown any shorter. While our personal circumstances and responsibilities will vary, most of us seem to be overwhelmed, distracted, short on sleep, and unable to determine how we spend our time. *Where did the day go?* we ask ourselves, when it seems to have gone by in a blur. We talk about trying to get more balance into our lives and of having some time to relax, relate in a meaningful manner, or just chill or dream. Sadly we seem to find this difficult to achieve, with the result that our lives seem contracted, and we're not in touch with how we really feel, and we're only superficially in touch with others in our lives.

Why is it that we get so busy, filling our diaries with events and commitments that seem to come round with astonishing rapidity? The answer is far from obvious. We need to get to know ourselves better to understand why. It may be because we want the excitement of living a full life; we're greedy for experiences. Or it may be because we want to surround ourselves with people because we're afraid of being alone and feeling empty. It's possible that we're driven by ambition for recognition or wealth, or even by someone else's expectation of our success. It could be that we're adrenaline junkies and have gotten used to riding the roller coaster and are afraid to try something different.

Whatever the reason, we're not going to be able to fathom it out and make changes unless we get to know ourselves really well. To do this we need to slow down and create a little space and quiet time that is ours alone. As Blaise Pascal, the seventeenth-century French theologian, claimed, "All men's miseries derive from being unable to sit quiet in a room." The twentieth-century writer and poet, May Sarton, wrote lyrically in her memoirs about the need for time alone—a full life for her was not her "real life" unless she had time alone to "taste it fully," to discover and explore what is happening, or has happened.

When we pay attention and train our minds to be focused, things are different. Periods of quiet are essential to our wellbeing. They help us think straight, sort out our feelings, digest what is going on, and dream of other possibilities. Sitting quietly helps us sort out our confusion and recharges the batteries.

I choose to slow down.

I am willing to take time to get to know myself better.

2. Paying attention

Sometimes our lives feel out of control. We're overwhelmed by the information coming at us from all directions—the thoughts, emotions, and sensations from inside us, and everything that is happening outside in the world around us. Connectivity may now be more of a curse than a blessing as we spend so much of our time on our phones and tablets that we fail to connect with people in the flesh. Is it any wonder we end up feeling drained and exhausted?

We use very little conscious attention in our daily lives. We get out of bed, shower, dress, prepare breakfast, take the children to school and ourselves to our place of work—all this automatically, without really needing to think about it. Our brains are so adept, we can even make judgments, adopt attitudes, make choices and decisions, remember things, and set goals without really concentrating. Paying full attention requires more work and energy.

The word "attention" comes from the Latin verb, *attendere*, meaning to stretch toward. When we pay attention to something, we stretch toward it, focus on it, excluding everything else that might distract us. As a result we begin to see it more clearly, hear it more distinctly, feel it, smell it, and taste it.

A Zen master was asked by a student to write down some significant words of wisdom. The master took his brush and wrote the word "Attention." The student was puzzled and asked him to write more. So he wrote "Attention. Attention." The student became irritable, and said that he failed to see what was so deep about that. The master then wrote the same word three times, "Attention. Attention. Attention." Angrily the student asked him what "Attention" meant. Gently the master replied, "Attention means attention."

Paying attention is an art. When we slow down and pay attention, everything changes. Controlled focus becomes like a laser beam, and with that focus the mind becomes peaceful and joy wells up from deep within us.

I'm reminded of my experience of learning to paint flowers. My teacher kept telling me, "If you can see, you can paint." You have to look closely at a flower—its petals, stamens, stem, and leaves, its colors and composition, the way the light falls, the relationship of one part to another, and, most importantly, the spaces between the parts.

Painting a picture, playing the piano, gardening, flower arranging, or making a loaf of bread all require focus and attention. There is no place for distracted thoughts. When we focus, everything else is forgotten except the task at hand. Our troubles are left behind, and we feel a sense of deep peace.

I am willing to pay attention.
I choose to focus on my breathing.

3. Taming the unruly mind

If we are busy, our minds are even busier. There's an incessant flow of thoughts running through our brains. The average person is estimated to have in the region of 60,000 thoughts in a day. It's hardly surprising we feel tired!

If we remain still and quiet for any length of time, without any distractions, we become aware of this endless stream of thoughts. The trick is not to allow them to besiege us and get caught up in the maelstrom, but rather to learn to accept them and let them go. We can learn to control our minds and train our attention through the practice of mindfulness, meditation, yoga, tai chi, and other numerous disciplines and techniques.

"To know that you are a prisoner of your mind is the dawn of wisdom," claimed the Indian sage, Nisargadatta Maharaj. Taming our minds requires that we remain still and be present. Focusing on the breath is the most natural and simplest of ways to begin training. Our breath is always with us, we don't need anything else, and we certainly don't have to have any particular beliefs. By paying attention to the breath as it goes in and out of our nostrils, and watching how even with this simplest of exercises, the mind constantly wanders, we begin to see just how much we are in the clutches of the mind. However, as we bring our attention back to the breath, our breathing rhythm begins to change, gradually slowing as each inhalation and exhalation lengthens, and we notice that the thoughts begin to subside. Over time we begin to become more self-aware, and we can use attention to empower our lives and to get to know ourselves better.

Gradually we are able to regain that deep sense of peace that the inspirational self-study course *A Course in Miracles* aims to help us achieve:

Developing awareness

There is a silence
into which the world cannot intrude.
There is an ancient peace
you carry in your heart
and have not lost.

I accept my thoughts and release them.

I pay attention to breathing in and breathing out.

I choose peace.

4. Adopting mindfulness

Mindfulness is about being awake. It's not a practice that requires adherence to any particular religious or esoteric belief, but it is a universal way of becoming more aware. According to Jon Kabat-Zinn at the University of Massachusetts Medical Center, who has pioneered the research on the subject, "Mindfulness is the art of conscious living."

We tend to live our lives in an unconscious manner much of the time, preoccupied with the past or the future, and not living in the present moment. When we are mindful, however, our automatic patterns of thinking and behaving begin to break up,

and we start to see things in a new way. Our perceptions shift and we experience the world as we first
did in our earliest years before we were conditioned
to experience fear and limitation.

Mindfulness helps make us more aware. We can
choose to take responsibility for our lives by taking
responsibility for our thoughts. The Buddha claimed:
"What we are today comes from our thoughts of
yesterday, and our present thoughts build our life
tomorrow: our life is the creation of our mind."

So how do we become mindful? There are two
approaches. One is by thinking in a more flexible
way, by actively keeping the mind open to both
uncertainty and possibility. Ellen Langer, Professor
of Social Psychology at Harvard, pioneered this
approach and advocated avoiding all automaton-like
behavior where we are basically "mindless." Instead,
increasing mindfulness, breaking loose from old
mindsets and paying attention, and staying open to
intuition, enables us to see clearly and deeply. In the
following lines from "Tintern Abbey," the poet William Wordsworth's "quiet eye" shows how intuition
and mindfulness are reached by escaping the usual
single-minded focus of life lived on autopilot:

> While with an eye made quiet by the power
> of harmony, and the deep power of joy,
> we see into the life of things.

Developing awareness

The other approach to becoming more mindful is one that is becoming increasingly fashionable. Jon Kabat-Zinn at the UMass Medical Center pioneered the practice of mindfulness, drawing on the practice of Buddhist meditation. Professor Mark Williams at the University of Oxford has popularized a non-religious mindfulness as a method of training the mind. The idea is that we can meditate anywhere, for a few minutes or longer. Stopping, sitting, and becoming aware of the breath are suggested as a daily practice. This enables us to have a more mindful awareness as we go about our daily lives and encourages us to break our unconscious habits of thinking and behaving. When we bring our awareness to breathing, the shift in attention reminds us that we are here now, and we feel connected to the life force as the breath goes in and out of the body. The idea is to carry over mindfulness into everyday life while we're cooking, eating, ironing, cleaning, etc. It helps us see things as they are, not as we expect them to be, or how we want them to be, or how we fear they might become.

Both forms of mindfulness result in a greater overall wellbeing when practiced regularly. They have been found to lower blood pressure, slow down the release of stress hormones, and increase the levels of the neuro-hormones dopamine, melatonin, and serotonin. They appear to aid the immune system to function better, helping us fight illness and slowing down the aging process. In addition, mindfulness helps us live with greater awareness, have a different perspective on life, and a greater appreciation of the world around us.

I can take responsibility for my thoughts.
I am willing to let go of fear and limiting beliefs.

5. Practicing meditation

If we want to be in touch with who we really are and to find the Source of joy within ourselves, meditation is an important tool. Although there are many techniques and practices, the essence of meditation is the training of our mind to settle into a state of calmness and clarity.

The simplest of all meditations is to focus on the breath. We sit in an upright but relaxed posture, we close our eyes, and we watch the breath as it goes in and out of our nostrils. The breath connects us both with what's inside us and the current of life that flows through everything that exists. As we focus on the incoming and outgoing flow of our breath, not only does our breath slow down, but also the rush of thoughts begins to subside as we gently acknowledge whatever thought has arisen and then let go of it.

It's not complicated, but it's also not easy to stay with the practice. It requires effort to remain focused. The sound of a lawn mower reminds us that the grass needs cutting, and then we remember that we meant to get the mower serviced. We like the man who owns the service shop but his wife was definitely a bit discourteous with us the last time we met her. We wonder what the reason for that was; maybe she's not happy. Our sister isn't happy because her husband's just left her—must go and see her . . . and so it goes on, our mind wanders all over the place, one thought leading to another, until we realize we've digressed from our simple practice of focusing on the breath.

However, we keep returning to the breath, bringing our awareness gently back to the practice. If we can just observe what's happening rather than reacting, or labeling, or judging, then we will find that we have moments when the chatter ceases. Gradually we come to see how the mind behaves, and over time we begin to understand ourselves better. We start to see our patterns of thought, feeling, and behavior, what's actually going on under the surface. We also get to access the deep well of joy at the center of our being.

Meditation does require us to be disciplined. We have to find the time and space, we have to make a commitment to sit regardless of what is going on, and we have to stay with the breath. Over time we begin to reap the benefits of practice—our health and wellbeing, our energy levels, our ability to relax, our capacity for joy, our creativity, our relationships, all are improved with practicing meditation on a daily basis.

I observe what's happening rather than reacting.

I keep returning to the breath.

I allow myself to become calm.

6. Finding a place to retreat to

Having a place we can go to where we can be still and quiet, beyond the merry-go-round of our daily lives, is beneficial. Time to do nothing in particular, to potter around, or to engage in peaceful contemplation makes a big difference in how we feel. Although being alone with ourselves isn't always easy. We might be lucky enough to go on a formal retreat or take a break away from the city, or we might only be able to manage a walk in the park or public gardens. We might be fortunate enough to have a room that we can make our own, but if not, even a small corner of a room where we can make a dedicated space and sit quietly is fine.

Artists, writers, poets, and composers have testified to the vital importance of being alone and quiet. "Silence is the perfectest herald of joy," wrote Shakespeare in *Much Ado About Nothing*. Goethe was insistent that he could produce nothing "without absolute solitude." And as for Mozart: "When I am, as it were, completely myself, entirely alone, and of good cheer . . . it is on such occasions that ideas flow best and most abundantly."

Mystics have always understood the value of silence and solitude, retreating to the wilderness or the cloisters in a secluded place for meditation and contemplation. The Indian sage Ramana Maharshi wrote: "Silence is unceasing Eloquence. It is the best language." Richard Jefferies, the English mystic and writer, was ecstatic about his experience of being alone in nature: "I was utterly alone with the sun and the earth. Lying down on the grass, I spoke in my soul to the earth, the sun, the air, and the distant sea . . ."

Li Po (or Li Bai, as he was also known) was an acclaimed poet of the Tang dynasty in China and well understood the value of being in the wilderness:

> You ask why I make my home in the moun-
>   tain forest,
> and I smile, and am silent,
> and even my soul remains quiet:
> it lives in the other world
> which no one owns.
> The peach trees blossom.
> The water flows.

I know from my own experience of spending time in nature how restorative it can be. Away from the bustle of life in the city, in places of great scenic beauty, whether it's Yosemite National Park, the Lake District, or the Himalayas, I have felt a deep connection with the landscape, myself, and others, and have felt a sense of peace and joy. However, I can also experience this when I'm working in my garden, or when I retreat to the attic of our family home, where I have space to read, reflect, and practice meditation.

There's something about spending time in nature that makes us realize how magnificent creation is, and how a power greater than ourselves connects us all. The secret is to arrive at that same feeling through sitting on a cushion in one's own quiet space at home.

I make time and space to be alone.
I am connected to the Source of life.
I'm restored by the peace I find within.

7. Knowing ourselves—the journey inward

We all make two journeys through life. One is the obvious seven-part journey from infancy to old age, with all its various adventures and experiences unique to each of us. There is also the inner journey, the journey of self-knowledge, which is called by many names—the Way, the Path, the Tao.

"Know Thyself" was inscribed above the entrance to the shrine of Apollo at Delphi (interestingly this was originally a shrine to Gaia, the earth goddess, before the advent of patriarchal religion). The maxim was also used in the writings of Plato, Socrates, and Aeschylus, as well as by later philosophers like Hobbes and Rousseau, and poets like Emerson and Coleridge.

Rumi, the thirteenth-century Persian theologian, mystic, and poet, described how we keep looking outside ourselves for answers when all the time, the answer is within us:

The Guest was in the house but we, like
    lunatics
were running in the streets searching for
    him
"I am here! He kept calling from inside
while we like doves kept cooing,
"Where, where are you?"

Knowing ourselves is vital. No one can know us as well as we know ourselves and yet we tend to unwittingly conceal our real selves. We have an image of ourselves that was formed in childhood and was modified as we grew into adulthood, but that's not who we truly are. Our authentic self may be quite different from the image we project. This image is based on perceptions that are no longer relevant, and our patterns of behavior are often driven by the need for approval, a need to be loved, or a need to fit in.

As the writer and activist Alice Walker wrote, "The most foreign country is within." We have to get to know this strange land by being willing to explore the depths of ourselves. This journey inward is both psychological and spiritual. When we look within we develop greater awareness as we observe ourselves behaving in certain ways. We begin to understand our emotions and thoughts, and have insights as to why they are the way they are. Gradually, through techniques like mindfulness and meditation, we can bring them under conscious control and make changes and adjustments, so that our lives seem to run more harmoniously and become richer and more meaningful. We feel a sense of being connected to something greater than ourselves, yet there's a soft-ness at our center that allows us to be more open-hearted—both to ourselves and to others. It doesn't mean that our lives become free of problems, but it does mean that we are able to give depth and value to our experiences of everyday life.

I let go of the false image I have of myself.
I am willing to find my authentic self.
I love myself and all that I am.

8. Listening to our intuition

The ancient Greeks believed that intuition was attributable to the gods; the psychologist C. G. Jung thought it came from the collective unconscious, an inherited form of the unconscious that we all share and that is different from our own individual unconscious; and the biologist Rupert Sheldrake postulates that it may have to do with morphic resonance—the idea that memory is inherent in nature. Whatever the explanation, intuition is not something possessed by a few people, but a sense that we all share. Those gut feelings, hunches, and premonitions that we experience from time to time, or the vivid dreams that stay with us, are all intuition speaking to us.

The word "intuition" derives from the Latin *intueri*, meaning to look upon, consider, or contemplate. It's something that we see, hear, or feel that makes available to us the unlimited knowledge and wisdom that we have access to. The psychologist Marcia Emery has described it as being "like a satellite dish that picks up signals in the form of images, ideas, and feelings and beams them onto the screen of your conscious awareness."

When we perceive the messages of intuition in this non-rational way, we need to be open to accepting them. We can silence a vital message by evaluating new information on rational grounds. The subconscious part of ourselves is signaling to us something the conscious self does not know. This enables us to gain insight into, and understanding of, our past, and to provide solutions for the future.

We all have the capacity for intuition to a greater or lesser extent, and we can develop it further. It's rather like the way we use muscles in our bodies— they work better the more we use them. The more we work to develop our intuition, the more it can help us in every aspect of our lives, whether in communicating with others, making decisions, or getting the creative juices flowing. Too often we look to others for guidance, but intuition enables us to find answers for ourselves. The answers are already there deep within us. We just need to sit, wait, and listen.

I sit and listen.

I am open to receiving the messages of intuition.

I trust that the answers to my questions are deep within me.

9. Revealing ourselves in our intimate relationships

If we want to share genuinely intimate relationships, we need to be prepared to reveal who we truly are. Developing our awareness helps us to achieve this, because when we know how we really feel and are able to talk about it clearly and coherently others can understand us better.

Often we're afraid to reveal our emotions because we're attached to a particular image we have of ourselves. This image has been influenced by family and significant people in our lives, as well as the society in which we live. We've learned how to survive in relationships by unconsciously allowing certain traits and qualities to manifest, and by inhibiting others. We also tend to fear the consequences of being honest—we're reluctant to expose ourselves to possible anger or impatience, and don't want to be subjected to criticism or possible ridicule.

We need to be able to talk about things that are important to us, however, even when the other person thinks and feels somewhat differently. We also need to be able to share our hopes and dreams about the future. We have to be who we really are, rather than what the other person wishes or needs us to be.

At the same time as staying true to our own beliefs and values, we need to respect the other person's. We need to understand that closeness doesn't equal sameness. Rainer Maria Rilke, one of the German language's greatest twentieth-century poets, put it beautifully:

> Once the realization is accepted that even between the closest human beings infinite distances continue to exist, a wonderful living side by side can grow up, if they succeed in loving the distance between them which makes it possible for each to see the other whole against the sky.

We have to allow the other person to be who they are, and not expect them to be who we want them to be, consciously listening to what they're saying and giving them time to speak without interjecting. It's no mean feat to stay connected emotionally when there is disagreement, whilst at the same time staying true to ourselves. There's no way we should expect to be able to change someone, nor is it a good idea to blame or criticize. It's far better to find things in the other person to appreciate, whilst at the same time remaining clear about any behavior that is unacceptable

Truthful and skillful communication requires pauses and restraint, so that there is time to think about what we're saying and say it clearly. We also need to listen not just to what is said by the other person before we reply, but also to the tone of voice, and to watch facial expressions and gestures. We also need to pay attention to how we're reacting.

Ultimately our intimate relationships will benefit from how well we know ourselves and how willing we are to look at ourselves honestly. Above all we need to have a profound respect for difference.

I have the confidence to be myself.

I allow others to be themselves.

I respect the difference between myself and others.

10. Showing respect in all our relating

Good relationships in all areas of our lives certainly result in greater happiness, with health benefits too. There is evidence that those who enjoy good relationships tend not to get sick very often and also are inclined to live longer. Loneliness, by contrast, increases the risk of everything from depression to heart attacks, dementia, and death.

We are all more similar than we imagine. It doesn't matter what sex, age, background, race, or religion we are, deep down we all want the same thing—to be happy and avoid suffering. I'm reminded of a photo I saw recently of one brown egg and one white, with a caption—"the yolk is the same." We're all the same on the inside.

However, because of who we think we are, our perceptions and beliefs, our likes and dislikes, and our habits and the distinctions we make, we tend to see ourselves as more separate than the same. And yet, within all of us is that spark of divinity. It is that spark that we need to honor. We show respect by being open and warm, by being considerate and compassionate, remembering the common humanity we share.

We can listen consciously to what people have to say in a situation, and we can be mindful of how we react. Skillful communication is always preferable to reacting without thinking. If there's friction, it's better to view the situation as a challenge to work on ourselves, refraining from blame and criticism. If we can find something to appreciate in the other person and make them feel good about themselves, greater harmony is bound to be the result.

I know that we're all the same on the inside.
I honor the spark of divinity in everyone.

Chapter III

Letting go of negative emotions

*We know what we feel,
know what we desire,
then slowly surrender
to accept what is, and forgive.
What might have been
the salt of bitterness
becomes the salt of wisdom.*

MARION WOODMAN

Letting go of negative emotions is essential if we want to have more joy in our lives. We all experience a broad range of emotions, but negative emotions like fear, anger, envy, resentment, guilt, and shame emerge when life doesn't go the way we want it, which it rarely does. Such emotions can be problematic and prevent us from experiencing true joy. Whereas positive emotions like love, openness, courage, and empathy enhance life and health, negative emotions create tension and stress.

The origin of negative emotions lies in our past. We have forgotten what was effectively programmed into our brains in childhood and have remained as misperceptions in our thinking. It's our thoughts that create emotions, and we need to understand how we unconsciously hold on to these limiting thoughts and beliefs. We tend to think we are our emotions, when they are simply feelings—they are not who we are. Only when we become more aware of our thoughts can we begin to see them for what they are and let them go.

When our needs are being met in life, positive thoughts and feelings follow. When they're not met, then our thoughts turn judgmental, defensive, and protective. Often we try to suppress uncomfortable emotions, or we may do the opposite, giving vent to them and behaving inappropriately. There's much that we cannot control in life, but our minds can learn to control the thoughts we have, and thus our behavior. We can choose to think differently and let go.

Perhaps we can think of it as akin to taking a train. We put our luggage in the rack, sit down and relax, knowing the luggage will get transported. We don't need to hang on to it during the journey. Likewise, all we need do if we feel burdened is to let go of what's weighing us down.

When we learn to release and consciously let go of negative thoughts and feelings, we free ourselves from the misguided patterns of behavior that no longer serve us. We can forgive ourselves for our mistakes, and then more easily forgive others, recognizing that though they may have hurt us, they too have their own difficult paths.

Forgiveness can be a real challenge. We need to work hard to understand the reasons behind the behavior of someone who has wronged us. The Native Americans say that to truly understand someone, we have to walk in their moccasins. All the religious traditions of the world have emphasized the need for forgiveness. Forgiveness is always in our best interests—we forgive, or we continue to suffer. Healing only begins when forgiveness and reconciliation take place.

We always have the freedom to choose, taking charge of our minds and emotions. Just beneath the surface of emotion, joy already exists. When we let go of what's burdening us, we allow the joy within to flow unimpeded. It's like releasing a kink in a hosepipe so that the water can easily flow again.

1. Dropping our emotional baggage

Life is difficult, but not as difficult as we think it is. As the Chinese proverb says: "You cannot prevent the birds of sorrow flying over your head, but you can prevent them from building nests in your hair."

We actually make our lives harder by holding on to long-held beliefs and self-imposed limitations that are not appropriate. As children we wanted love and approval from our parents, and as we grew up, from our teachers and peers. We learned how to get our needs met by adopting certain patterns of behavior, and these became habits. Gradually we created a self-image, and in order to make sense of our lives, we told ourselves stories about who we were, and we continue to do this, modifying and justifying that self-image that is our identity.

By becoming more aware of these stories we tell ourselves and the roles we play automatically that cause us unhappiness, we can begin to let go of them. We need to take an honest look at our past in order to understand, leaving behind the hurts, fears, and disappointments of our earlier years. Whatever happened is in the past, and we need to accept that the wounds were inflicted, but there is no need to keep revisiting them and suffering.

We always have a choice about what our thoughts dwell on as Rumi, the Persian mystic and poet of the thirteenth century, cautioned us:

Stop walking in your own shadow
wallowing in your foolish thoughts.
Raise your head, look at the sun, walk
among the flowers, become a human being.

We can let the circumstances of our life close us down, or we can let them open us up. We can let go of our negative thoughts. By becoming more aware of the patterns that run through our lives, we can change what we believe is who we are. Once we see ourselves more clearly we can begin to accept and love ourselves. We can also reshape our stories to give us what we most want out of life for the future.

❧

I release beliefs that are no longer appropriate.
I let go of the past.
I accept and love myself.

2. Accepting what we can and can't control

The Roman Stoic, Epictetus, who was born a slave but became a great philosopher-teacher, opened his manual on living with a fundamental truth: "Some things are within our control, and some things are not." What we think and feel is always within our control—we always have a choice. It's only external things like the body we're born with, other people, the weather, and unexpected events that we have no control over.

Trying to control our lives results in frustration and misery, but taking responsibility for our lives means we are more able to deal with what confronts us. In everyday life, we hate the feeling of everything getting on top of us. Too many demands on us, major problems that overwhelm us and minor issues that need our attention, mean that we cannot see the wood for the trees and we end up worrying. We lie awake at 4:00 a.m. wondering what to do, and then drag ourselves out of bed in the morning to face another day—burned out and exhausted.

We worry about what people think of us, but looking to others for validation only works temporarily; we worry about what we think we ought to achieve, but these may be others' goals, not ours; we worry about the future and how it might unfold. Worrying, however, is nothing more than an attempt to control our lives. And it is pointless, because we miss living in the present moment and are closed to the possibilities before us. We end up missing the joy that is available to us each and every day.

The solution is to stop trying to micromanage every detail of our lives and the lives of those who are part of it. We need to let go of the constant need to try to control what we cannot control and focus on what we can. As the Serenity Prayer by Reinhold Niebuhr reminds us: "God grant me the serenity to accept the things I cannot change, the courage to change the things I can, and the wisdom to know the difference."

Why not make a list of your worries—and then shred it!

I take responsibility for my life.

I let go of worrying.

I accept what I cannot change.

3. Realizing we don't need to be perfect

Many of us try too hard to meet impossible perfect standards. We always want to know the answers, do everything right, and never make mistakes. We try to look well-dressed, stylish, and attractive, to be professional and efficient in our careers, to be good mothers, considerate partners, dutiful daughters, pillars of the community, etc. So busy trying to attain perfection and hold everything together, we become rigid and inflexible, losing touch with what we're thinking and feeling, and less able to genuinely connect with others.

We're too hard on ourselves. We're not indispensable, and we're not perfect—we're human, with all our faults and flaws, and our life is a work in progress. Instead of beating ourselves up for failing to meet our high standards, we need to congratulate ourselves on what we have achieved. We need to be kinder to ourselves. Self-acceptance is one of the most important factors in producing a consistent sense of well-being.

Underlying the need for perfection is fear. We're driven to do better because we fear we're not good enough and before long we'll be found out. I struggled with this in my own past. Only with hindsight did I understand that I drove myself too hard in my corporate life because of the fear of failure. I paid a price for this in terms of my marriage, which I neglected in focusing on my need to succeed. But ultimately I learned from the experience, and realized the necessity of letting go of the requirement to be perfect.

Some are less fortunate, and lives can spiral into chaos when feelings of inadequacy and failing to make the grade become overwhelming, resulting in depression, addiction, and, in extreme cases, suicide. Rachel Gow was a twenty-nine-year-old career girl who killed herself because she didn't want to turn thirty without a husband and children. It is tragic that she gave up because she was not where she thought she ought to be in life, when in fact she had everything to live for.

The pressures on young women in particular to succeed now are intense. Not only do they have to have a successful career, but they should be getting married, buying a house, having children . . . the biological clock is ticking! In addition, social media, where many portray themselves as having such a perfect time, exacerbates expectations.

We all need to relax and let go of this crazy idea of the need for perfection. If we can slow down and take time out to reflect on our lives, we can appreciate where we are and what we have. If we stop worrying about what everyone else is doing, we can be happier, and our lives become less stressful.

❦

I recognize that my life is a work in progress.

I let go of the need to be perfect.

I appreciate where I am and what I have in my life.

4. Managing stress

Stress is part of life, but as the world has become ever more complex with our digital lifestyles and the expectation of availability 24/7, we're finding it increasingly difficult to process. Whether we're trying to deal with the daily demands from our family or work, whether it's the unexpected bolt from the blue like an illness or an accident, or a significant life event like a wedding, or simply traffic congestion, deadlines, and arguments, emotional stress manifests as impatience, anxiety, fear, frustration, or anger.

Stress isn't totally bad—it can actually have some positive aspects. Stress floods the body with hormones including adrenaline, noradrenaline, and cortisol that prime us to deal with danger (its original purpose being to get us ready for fight or flight when threatened). Some stress comes from exciting new experiences. It is also important in that it can force us to change and grow. However, long-term negative stress, where we're constantly overreacting, is damaging to our quality of life and our health.

We endeavor to cope with negative stress in all sorts of ways, from denial to a whole range of addictive behaviors, but these are detrimental ways of dealing with stress and only temporarily ease the discomfort. When we're stressed, the powerful cascade of chemicals rushes into our bodies from our brains, manifesting in shallow breathing, rapid heartbeat, sweating, and even full-blown panic attacks. If we carry on responding to stress in the same habitual ways, these symptoms result in high blood pressure, ulcers, strokes, and heart attacks. We know this from the growing body of scientific evidence, which demonstrates the long-term effects of stress on our health.

Although our lives are inherently stressful since we cannot control what happens, we can change the way we perceive, react, and adapt to stressful situations. The positive way of dealing with stress is to start responding to it, rather than reacting as if we're fighting for our lives. We need to decide to do things differently, recognizing the signs and looking at what's going on inside. Remembering that we have choices, we can close our eyes and be still, allowing the thoughts, feelings, and sensations to surface. Breath work, relaxation techniques, yoga, tai chi, mindfulness, meditation, Emotional Freedom Technique, and image work or visualization all help to ameliorate symptoms and enable us to reduce the tensions we're experiencing. We can replace negative emotions with positive ones, literally rewiring our brains to send different chemical signals to our bodies.

The healing power that we unleash in a positive mental state has been confirmed by cardiologists working at the HeartMath Institute in Boulder Creek, California. They have found that positive emotions create increased harmony and coherence in heart rhythms and improve balance in the nervous system.

I choose to respond differently to stress.

I can replace negative emotions with positive ones.

5. Becoming aware of the Shadow

"The Shadow" (a term coined by the great psychiatrist C. G. Jung) is the face we hide from the world. It's what we can't admit to or don't like about ourselves, the feelings that cause disquiet, or the behaviors our culture regards as wrong. When we're confronted with the Shadow aspects of ourselves it's rather like the experience of Dorian Gray in Oscar Wilde's *The Picture of Dorian Gray*. Ever youthful and perfect after his pact with the portrait painter, the narcissistic Dorian Gray sees the painting of himself that has been hidden away in a locked room. It shows, to his horror, all the signs of aging and degeneration that were there all along in his decadent life, but not evident in his face.

When we consign parts of ourselves that we fear or are ashamed of to the Shadow, they become part of our unconscious. We cannot face it in ourselves, and we cannot tolerate it in others either.

We create the Shadow, according to Jung, in early childhood when we construct an image of ourselves in order to be loved by our parents. We hide those parts of ourselves that they criticized and rebuked us for. As the years progressed, we also sought acceptance from our teachers and peers, and again continued to hide other unacceptable parts that did not fit our image. What we ended up with was the Persona, the face we present to the world.

In adulthood, the rejected parts of us are still buried below the surface and emerge from time to time to cause us pain and crisis in the form of self-destructive behavior, abuse, depression, anxiety, or shame. Jung maintained that we have to make the darkness conscious in order to become fully mature human beings.

If, through developing our awareness, we can come to see and understand the Shadow aspects of ourselves, and not judge them, and over time come to accept them, then we are less likely to be sabotaged by them. We come to know ourselves better and can manage our emotions and behavior with greater understanding. We are more able to present our authentic face to the world.

I acknowledge the rejected parts of myself.
I am able to be my authentic self.

6. Cultivating healthy expression of anger

It's perfectly normal to experience feelings of anger when life throws something at us that is painful or seems unfair. Emotional health means experiencing all our feelings, even the negative ones, but without becoming overwhelmed by them. Repressing or denying negative feelings isn't healthy, and unexpressed anger can lead to resentment and depression. That doesn't mean, however, that it's okay to either indulge in negative feelings or lose control and behave inappropriately.

We tend to get irritable or angry when we feel emotionally stressed, and it seems that we're all becoming angrier because we're experiencing more stress than ever before. Beneath the anger is a sense that our core values, beliefs, or goals are being threatened in some way. Women have historically been discouraged from expressing anger. Rather, it's our job to keep the peace, to nurture, and to please! As a result, we tend to either vent our anger ineffectively, complaining and blaming, or we feel we cannot express it and bottle it up inside ourselves. While unexpressed anger can lead to depression and ill health, uncontrolled anger that is threatening, bullying, or vengeful is dangerous and destructive, and in such cases anger management courses can be helpful.

Anger can actually be useful when used in a measured way as a tool for change in relationships. It can also be harnessed creatively by being channeled into some worthwhile cause like social or environmental reform. How we express our anger is what matters, and how long we stay mad. We need to understand why we are angry and to learn to communicate clearly and effectively the reason for our anger. Ideally, it's been suggested, anger shouldn't last for longer than ninety seconds. Any longer, and all we're doing is replaying the story, going over the same ground.

By being able to manage our fears and communicate our angry feelings, we can grow and become more emotionally mature, and our relationships are enriched. Communication is vital, as the poet William Blake expresses here:

I was angry with my friend:
I told my wrath, my wrath did end.
I was angry with my foe:
I told it not, my wrath did grow.

If we can stay present and aware when we're feeling angry, then we can slow down potentially explosive situations instead of reacting inappropriately, and are far more likely to be able to handle things skillfully. Ultimately, we need to be able to transmute negative feelings like anger into understanding and compassion.

I communicate the anger I feel clearly and effectively.
I manage my fears and handle difficult situations skillfully.

7. Eliminating envy

We experience a whole range of feelings, but they are just that—feelings, no more than bubbles, and *we are not our feelings*. We hold on to feelings that arise and forget that they are only feelings and that we're holding on to them, and when they are negative, they harm not only others but ourselves too.

Envy is a pointless yet poisonous emotion, and detrimental to our health. It's basically about lack, and what we want and don't have. We don't feel satisfied with our lives as they are and rarely enjoy what we do have. We envy others their good fortune and wish we could have what they have—it could be their looks, their wealth, their partner and children, their lovely home, or their success. It's a kind of madness because things are often not as they seem, or if they are, sooner or later they change anyway.

A young and attractive friend of mine seemingly had the "perfect life." Married to a wealthy man whom she adored, with two lovely daughters and a beautiful home and garden, she enjoyed a wonderful lifestyle. One day, however, her husband was racing his Ferrari and had an accident. He died soon after. My friend was devastated. Fortunately, after a few years she was able to rebuild her life.

Another friend was looking forward to her husband's retirement because they had all sorts of plans to travel and generally enjoy life. Sadly, he had a massive heart attack, and not long after she developed breast cancer. And yet another friend lost her young son while he was on holiday abroad. Sooner or later, we all have our share of misfortune, however rosy our lives may look from the outside or at a certain point in time.

When we feel lack in our lives, it's because we tend to assume that we have to struggle to get what we want, rather than letting the flow of life unfold for us with all its richness. It's our own belief in lack and limitation that holds us back. Resistance tends to stop us from having, doing, and being what we want in life, some old pattern that we're not yet fully aware of. We focus on our lack, rather than on the abundance of the Universe. We are contracted instead of feeling a sense of possibility and expansion.

If the feeling of envy arises, it's not that we should suppress it, but rather that we need to recognize and acknowledge it, and then choose to release it. When we let go of a negative emotion, it's like releasing the valve on a pressure cooker. We can let go of wanting things to be different and change things if we're not happy with our lives. And if we cannot, then we need to accept that it's not possible. We need to appreciate everything we do have in our lives and rejoice in others' good fortune and happiness, wishing them well.

I let go of any sense of lack and choose abundance.
I have everything I need.
I rejoice in others' good fortune.

8. Banishing guilt and shame

Guilt and shame are two other negative emotions that we sometimes have to deal with. The feelings are similar, though not identical, and can cause much unnecessary suffering, robbing us of peace of mind. Guilt says, "I have done something wrong," whereas shame says, "I am wrong."

Both feelings are associated with fear. The belief that one is guilty is usually accompanied by an expectation of punishment, conscious or unconscious, justified or unjustified. Shame is more insidious, because we feel we cannot talk to anyone about how bad we feel about ourselves inside.

In experiencing guilt or shame, we are in effect holding on to the past, and neither attempting to suppress the emotion nor punishing ourselves works. We hurt ourselves by dwelling on the past and going over the events again and again, and by being unable to live in the present moment. We need to tell ourselves that the past is over and done and cannot be changed. What can be changed, however, is our choice to let go and take responsibility for these feelings rather than be victimized by them.

We have to be willing to open up, to identify and express what has been stored inside in order to release these negative emotions. We may need help from a psychotherapist to do this if the original events have been particularly damaging and traumatic. Ultimately, we can release guilt or shame by telling ourselves that we've been punished enough. Self-acceptance and forgiveness of the mistakes we've made free us to make different choices and get on with fully living our lives.

I let go of the past.
I forgive myself.
I accept myself and love myself.

9. Forgiving ourselves and others

As human beings we make mistakes and say and do things we wish we hadn't done, or don't say and do things it might have been better to have said and done. We need to become aware of the fears, resentments, and judgments that underlie our behavior. Instead of condemning these feelings and being hard on ourselves, we need to be gentler with ourselves and accept them, whilst at the same time trying to change our patterns of behavior. If we've behaved badly toward someone, we need to let them know that we're sorry for the pain we've caused. We can choose to take responsibility instead of trying to put the blame elsewhere. This frees us and helps us to change our behavior, reclaiming our power and integrity rather than continuing to suffer.

We also need to be able to forgive others. We have to let go of old wounds, disappointments, and betrayals. Until there is forgiveness we are prisoners of the past and, therefore, unavailable to experience fully the present and the future. Lewis B. Smedes, a famous Christian author, wrote: "To forgive is to set a prisoner free and discover that the prisoner was you."

We need to cease being the victim, and stop replaying the tape of the story we told ourselves about what happened, causing us to feel the pain of the original wound over and over again. Instead of our hearts being closed down with sadness, bitterness, and thoughts of revenge, we have to let go and forgive. Holding on to resentment and anger only makes us continue to suffer and remain a prisoner. This doesn't mean that we condone the other person's behavior. We can forgive without denying what has been done; we can be reconciled without taking the other person back into our lives as if nothing ever happened. In the end, we forgive for our own peace of mind so that we can learn to move on and so that the other party can also move on. As the philosopher Hannah Arendt wrote, an act of forgiveness is "a constant mutual release."

In the case of horrific acts like murder, rape, sexual abuse, oppression, or acts of terror, it is far more difficult to forgive, and again we may require the help of a psychotherapist. There is always a choice, however, of whether to hang on to hatred and feelings of revenge forever, or to actively find a way of healing the wounds. Many do succeed in transforming their pain into forgiveness, but forgetting may be prerequisite before forgiveness is possible. Distance is necessary in order not to think about something terrible that happened every moment of the day. It is also necessary for any idea of vengeance to be given up before there can be any sense of freedom.

There is a story about two Buddhist monks who had been prisoners and been mistreated and tortured. At a later date when they had been released, one of them asked the other whether he had forgiven his captors. The second monk said, "Never!" To which the other monk replied, "Then I guess you will always be a prisoner."

I take responsibility for my behavior.
I choose forgiveness.

10. Healing and becoming whole

Healing is a process of becoming more whole, becoming consciously one with everything and feeling a sense of peace. The word "heal" derives from the Old English root "hal," to make whole, to bring together. As a yoga enthusiast, it reminds me of what the word "yoga" means, which is to yoke together, or union. Union with the Source of life is the object of yoga.

When we experience a sense of connection, understanding that we are part of a larger whole, we see ourselves and our problems differently. Our perspective shifts from fragmentation and isolation to wholeness or union. We no longer feel helpless and out of control, but begin to see possibilities and have a sense of acceptance of how things are. We can let go of stress and pain and experience peace of mind.

We often feel split as human beings, as different impulses, desires, aspirations, and principles struggle within us. We can also feel alienated because of past experiences. All our thoughts, memories, and wounds are literally embodied in us, stored in our muscles, tissues, and bones. Emotional pain trapped in our bodies can result in physical illness if it's not released. Our bodies are always communicating with us—the headache, the pain in our stomach, back, or neck, even the tiredness—are all trying to tell us something. If we don't heed the signals, then illness is likely to force us to rest and recover.

We have the capacity to heal ourselves. Healing does not mean "curing," rather it implies the possibility for us to relate differently to whatever it is we're confronting, whether it be illness, a horrific trauma, or even death itself. We can release the emotional pain we're experiencing by facing it, accepting it, and letting it go—there is no need to hang on to it. Understanding, releasing negativities, and forgiving ourselves and others, whilst at the same time being gentle with ourselves, are vital in the life-long process of becoming more whole.

I accept things as they are.
I let go of the pain I'm feeling.
I am becoming more whole.

11. Surrendering our expectations

Our lives are subject to forces beyond our control, and things have a tendency to not always turn out as we had hoped or planned. As the psychotherapist

Virginia Satir put it: "Life is not the way it's supposed to be. It's the way it is. The way you cope with it is what makes the difference."

However, this doesn't mean we shouldn't have dreams and plans for the future. Having the ambition to do well at college, to succeed in our chosen profession, to be an accomplished musician or artist, or to teach or serve in some way is using the gifts we've been given.

The Bible makes clear the need to not neglect our talents nor be afraid to use them in Jesus's Parable of the Talents. A man of property was leaving to go abroad and entrusted three of his servants with eight talents (a large sum of money) between them, according to their abilities. On his return he asked the servants what they had done with the money. The servant who had been given five talents had put the money to work and doubled its value, as had the second servant with his two talents, and they both gave the money to their master, who commended them. The third servant had buried his talent in the ground in order to keep it safe, but was castigated by the master for failing to use it.

As human beings we have to use our talents to the best of our abilities, but at the same time we need to be realistic about what may be possible. We have to be flexible when things don't go the way we want.

Although we need to put effort into something we want to accomplish, we need to take care that this is not to the exclusion of everything else in our lives. If we are overly ambitious, over-extended, ruthless in trying to attain our hopes and desires, and if we neglect our relationships, then we may find ourselves alone, out of balance, and feeling empty.

We need to let go of expectations of both ourselves and others. Whilst trying to be the best we can be, we also need to be aware that achieving the impossible is not a "should," especially when it impoverishes the rest of our lives. Neither can we have expectations of others that they behave as we do, or that they support us, regardless of their own needs, in our ambitions.

We cannot control things, they do not go according to plan, the unexpected always happens. We just do the best we can, accepting what we cannot change. Whatever our intentions, ultimately we always have to surrender to the power of the Universe and let go of the outcome.

I am flexible.
I release unrealistic expectations.
I surrender to the power of the Universe.

12. Decluttering our lives and minds

How cluttered our lives can become! There's too much stuff in our closets to see what to put on in the morning, there are too many emails to determine our priorities, too many boxes of this or that shoved into the attic so that we've no idea what's up there, or too many untried recipes torn out of magazines and pushed into a folder to decide what to cook. We tend to put sorting our clutter off until we're forced to do it because of a house move—because it all seems too overwhelming to deal with.

Clutter is both a symptom and a cause of stress, and we end up feeling there are just too many items on our to-do list, too many demands on our precious time, and too many days filled with commitments. We're also likely to feel besieged by too many thoughts in our heads.

When there is clutter, life energy cannot flow. We need to streamline our priorities. Once we can find a way to sort our personal clutter and maintain order (basically, starting in a small way, gradually clearing what we can, and continuing to cull on a regular basis) we will feel a greater sense of calm.

In the same way, we can get rid of stress-causing thoughts from our minds, saying goodbye to them just as we look at an old possession we no longer need and give it away. We are deeply affected by our thoughts, and we give them a significance they don't merit simply because they are there. We play and replay past scenarios, and we worry about the future and possible disasters that will probably never happen. We don't need all this distraction. We have the capacity to eliminate these thoughts and think differently. When it gets to overload point, we can call a halt. We can take a break and go for a walk, tidy up, bake a cake, or listen to some music—anything that helps us clear the mind and dissolve the distracting thoughts.

We can instead rewire our brains. We can change our automatic response patterns and substitute positive, life-affirming thoughts instead. We can use our imaginations to envisage a calm and decluttered life.

I free my life from clutter.
I release stress-causing thoughts.
I create a calm and decluttered life.

13. Facing up to our addictions

Addictive behavior is very prevalent in our society. It's not just the obvious addictions like alcohol and drugs, including prescription drugs, which we indulge in in the Western world, but also other addictions like food, money, work, shopping, social media, gambling, sex, and even TV or the gym. The dependency on our drug of choice is because at some level we're anxious, needy, depressed, lonely, or want to block something out. Our addictions alter our moods and mask our feelings. We are unaware of what is going on inside us, out of touch with our thoughts and feelings, and don't have to deal with the pain, anger, or confusion. The situation may not be helped either by a co-dependent family member or friend who participates in denial of the addiction because of their own immature needs.

The problem is that our addictions usually assuage the bad feelings at the time, but tend to only bring temporary relief until the next fix. Sadly, we've given up our power once we've become addicted to something. Only by facing it head on, and accepting that we have a problem, can we begin to tackle the craving for whatever it is we're addicted to. If we keep on running away from the painful feelings, we can't heal. We need to face them, not by judging ourselves, but by having patient understanding and compassion toward ourselves.

Serious addiction needs professional help, but for many of us, admitting that we're drinking probably more than we should be, or running up debt on our credit cards due to too much retail therapy, can be dealt with if we want to sort ourselves out without recourse to outside help. We just have to choose to address it.

It takes courage to look inside ourselves and deal with the thoughts and feelings we're grappling with. Gradually, however, we come to realize that the sense of wellbeing that we long for is deep inside us, not in that bottle of wine that seems to promise relaxation or yet another new dress that we think will make us look more attractive and desirable.

I am willing to release the need for my addiction.
I choose to face the painful feelings and let them go.
I know that I have a deep reservoir of joy within me.

Chapter IV

Cultivating optimism

The thought manifests as the word.
The word manifests as the deed.
The deed develops into habit.
And the habit hardens into character.
So watch the thought
and its ways with care.
And let it spring from love
born out of respect for all beings.

THE BUDDHA

Although some people seem to be born with a sunny disposition, many of us may have had to struggle with a tendency to see the glass as half empty. Throughout history, from the Greek philosopher Aristotle to modern-day motivational gurus like Anthony Robbins, the transformative power of optimism has been widely written about.

Researchers at the University of Illinois have reported that people who display a more optimistic attitude have significantly better cardiovascular health over the long term than those with a more pessimistic outlook. Evidence is now mounting that by constantly building our capacity to experience positive emotions we can actually alter our brains and experience greater wellbeing overall.

Life isn't easy—we live in an imperfect world and life isn't always fair, or so it would seem. No one appears to escape misfortune, loss, betrayal, or tragedy, neither are we exempt from setbacks and disappointments. How much we suffer is entirely up to us, however. We are not helpless, whatever life throws at us, for we can always choose our attitude. The English poet, Frederick Langbridge, conjured up a dramatic image:

> Two men look out through the same bars:
> One sees the mud, and one the stars.

We can choose not to be victims, and work consciously to balance the positive and negative. Our thoughts have the capacity to make us happy or sad, but we can change our thoughts and our behaviors, as the inspirational self-study course *A Course in Miracles* counsels: "You may believe that you are responsible for what you do, but not for what you think. The truth is that you are responsible for what you think, because it is only at this level that you can exercise choice. What you do comes from what you think."

First of all we need to accept that life is challenging. The world may be full of suffering, but we are also surrounded by much that is good and beautiful. If we open our eyes to all the wonders of life and focus on what we can appreciate, however bad our circumstances may be, we begin to feel less hopeless, and find learning new approaches and attitudes easier.

Optimists are aware that things can go wrong, but pessimists believe things will go wrong. Instead of worrying, optimists use their imagination to picture good things happening in the future, while pessimists keep going round in circles dwelling on the negative, which tends to become self-fulfilling.

When things go wrong, we have the opportunity to learn and grow, and can prevent similar things happening in the same way in the future. Karen Blixen (also known by her pen name Isak Dinesen), the Danish author famous for *Out of Africa*, wrote: "Difficult times have helped me to understand better than before how infinitely rich and beautiful life is in every way and that so many things that one goes worrying about are of no importance whatsoever."

We have to keep our minds focused on the positive, seeing the best in people and in situations if we are to live joy-filled lives. Life responds to us, so it's important to think and feel good as much as we possibly can. We can heed the advice of John Templeton, the highly successful investor and philanthropist, whose obituary in the *Wall Street Journal* was headlined "Maximum Optimist":

> There are three simple words that almost seem to have magical properties for developing a positive attitude in our life. *Feel supremely happy!* When you let yourself feel supremely happy—regardless of outer appearances—your whole body changes. Your thoughts, your facial expressions, your health, your attitudes, in fact, everything about you changes for the better.

1. Accepting life's challenges

Many years ago I was browsing in a bookshop, feeling decidedly low, when I had one of those *aha* moments. I had picked up *The Road Less Traveled*, destined back then to become a bestseller, by psychologist Scott Peck. His opening lines and what followed hit me with such force that I left the bookshop not only having purchased a copy of the book, but also with a lighter heart. His words made such sense to me and pointed to the way to end my difficulties:

Life is difficult.

This is a great truth, one of the greatest truths. It is a great truth because once we truly see this truth, we transcend it. Once we truly know that life is difficult—once we truly understand and accept it—then life is no longer difficult. Because once it is accepted, the fact that life is difficult no longer matters.

Sometimes it seems that life isn't just difficult—it's mean and cruel too. There will, however, always be tragedies, failures, and disappointments; fate strikes in unexpected and sometimes disastrous ways. The trick is to recognize that whatever has happened cannot be undone, but at the same time we can remain strong and balanced so that we are not thrown off-center by events. We can also regard the difficulties as challenges to help us grow.

The philosopher-psychologist William James, regarded as the father of the self-help movement, wrote in his *Principles of Psychology*: "Acceptance of what has happened is the first step in overcoming the consequences of any misfortune."

We always have choice—whether to be angry and seek revenge; whether to blame someone else and try to escape the pain through deadening and suppressing how we feel; or whether to engage in wishful thinking, wanting things to be other than they are. There's no point in dwelling on our problems because they then become magnified and can seem insurmountable. Accepting things as they are is the only thing that works and is the beginning of change. We have to face the situation head-on and be willing to consider new possibilities, which can bring hope and motivation. Only then can we learn from the experience, put it behind us, and move forward.

I see my difficulties as challenges to help me grow.

I accept that things are as they are.

I am willing to consider new possibilities.

2. Changing negative and limiting beliefs

We all have a set of beliefs we've arrived at through our past experiences. It's these beliefs that govern our behavior, and our feelings are the result of our beliefs. Many of these beliefs are negative, but they don't need to be. We can change them any time we want to. We can clear out the debris of indelible impressions left by our parents, siblings, teachers, and peers, as well as the experiences in general that have reinforced those impressions.

Neuroscience has proven that we can change our beliefs and attitudes by thinking differently. We can actually rewire our brains so that our habitual emotional reactions become a thing of the past. We can let go of our negative attitudes and refocus our energy with new beliefs, envisioning how we want our behavior to be.

We have to become self-aware. We do that by paying attention, and in the process we observe how our thoughts race around like a gaggle of unruly monkeys. We also observe that our thoughts are more negative than we realize. However, instead of labeling and judging them, we learn just to accept them and let them go.

Marcus Aurelius, one of the more enlightened of the Roman emperors, wrote: "Our life is what our thoughts make it."

When we transform our negative thinking and are motivated instead by positive emotions, our neural hardware gets rewired to reflect our thoughts as experience. Instead of producing a chain reaction of powerful chemicals in the brain that makes us feel emotionally stressed, when we have positive thoughts the chemical feedback makes us feel good. We feel the way we think, and then we think the way we feel!

Positive thoughts help us to feel expanded, loving, and grateful, and we feel differently about situations that previously made us unhappy. We come to see that there are many opportunities and possibilities for us to enrich our lives, as we sense the joy deep within us.

I can change my beliefs.

I am rewiring my brain with positive thoughts.

I embrace the opportunities to enrich my life.

3. Working with the Law of Attraction

We live on autopilot much of the time, and if something pleasant happens we're happy, and if something unpleasant happens we're unhappy. It doesn't have to be that way. Wayne Dyer, the well-known self-help author puts so succinctly: "When you change the way you look at things, the things you look at change."

Everything in the Universe vibrates and is magnetic, including feelings and thoughts. The Law of Attraction says that like attracts like, or we attract what we give out. In effect, we create our own reality through the magnetic frequency of our thoughts. The Law of Attraction is a concept found in many teachings and philosophies, but has been popularized over the last twenty years by the inspirational books of Esther and Jerry Hicks.

The mind is like a fast vibrating field of invisible energy, and our thoughts are constantly attracting our life experiences. If we think all is going great guns, we feel blessed, grateful, and happy—and we attract more of the same. Conversely, if we're feeling hard done by or miserable we only seem to attract negative situations that make us unhappier still. David Hawkins, the renowned psychiatrist and consciousness researcher, writes in *Power vs. Force:* "Every thought, action, decision, or feeling creates an eddy in the interlocking, interbalancing energy fields of life."

It makes sense, therefore, for us to do everything we can to be positive in our thoughts and to feel good. In effect, we need our mind to be operating at the higher energy frequencies of positivity.

We can imagine our life the way we want it to be, and most importantly, we need to imagine how it feels to be living that life. What we believe and feel is what will manifest in our lives, and it's important not to hold on to anything in our past that is negative and operates at lower energy frequencies. Ultimately, love is the highest vibrational frequency of the Universe, and that is what we need to choose above all else. As Rumi put it, "Love is the energizing elixir of the universe, the cause and effect of all harmonies." Love is nothing less than the life force that runs through us and everything in the Universe. When we choose the feeling of love and open-heartedness, we become positive and expansive, and when we don't, we are negative and contracted.

I think only positive thoughts, knowing that I will attract good things to me.

I let go of negativity.

I choose love and peace and joy.

4. Getting out of the rut

There are times in our lives when we feel "stuck" and need to get out of a rut. We feel trapped by circumstances—it might be an unhappy work situation, an abusive relationship, or a general lack of fulfillment in life. We seem to have lost ourselves beneath a plethora of demands, obligations, and responsibilities. We have no clarity about anything and have become anxious, even depressed. It doesn't matter if we get stuck from time to time, however, since it's an opportunity to find our way back home to our true selves. When we feel stuck life is trying to tell us something—we have to change.

We are never trapped irrevocably, though it might seem so. We always have the potential to change the ingrained patterns of thought and feeling that make us feel stuck. We need to be willing to change, and we only have to take that initial step and change one thing at a time.

An acquaintance of mine was happily married to a doctor with whom she had two small children and a nice home. The family was comfortable without the need to earn a second income. As time went by, she began to feel trapped, which resulted in depression. Gradually it dawned on her that she had given up her career for marriage and parenthood and, although she had no worries materially, she felt an emptiness and lack of fulfillment inside in spite of the other good things in her life.

She also realized that it was up to her to do something about her situation. So, whilst appreciating what was good about her life, she decided to take up a completely new interest in tapestry. She started working one day a week in a craft shop. Her world expanded and she became interested in arts and crafts, and ultimately art history. One thing led to another, but being prepared to examine how she felt, accepting it, and then taking that first step to change things got her out of the rut.

If we're stuck, we could all benefit from taking some time for ourselves to look closely at how we feel. Only then, when we realize what it is we're feeling, can we take steps to change our circumstances. Whilst still appreciating what we do have in life, we can begin to create more abundance and fulfilment in our lives.

I choose to change my ingrained patterns of thought.
I am willing to change my circumstances.
I choose to create abundance.

5. Retraining our brains

As long as our minds are disturbed we can't experience the joy inside ourselves. I like the Sufi metaphor of the body being like a carriage, the emotions like a horse, and the mind like the coachman. In our ordinary state of consciousness, the carriage is neglected and falls into disrepair. The horse is wild and uncontrolled, likely to bolt at the slightest provocation. The coachman is in the tavern, drinking with his friends. He has forgotten to feed the horse and oil the wheels of the carriage. The owner of the coach, therefore, never appears to ride in it. The moral of this little cameo is that the mind has to be sobered, the emotions tamed and trained, and the body has to be kept in good working order.

We have to learn to manage our minds and retrain our brains, just as much as we have to look after and exercise our bodies. To start with, we need to see what's going on in our minds. When our thoughts feel out of control, instead of letting them run us ragged, we need to stop and pay attention. We can observe the chatter, not label the thoughts or change them, but simply listen to them with awareness. A daily meditation practice helps retrain the mind, body, and brain. We begin to feel connected, whole, and balanced, and can see our lives more clearly; we feel calmer and more at peace.

If meditation practice seems an impossibility, then taking time to do something practical like going for a walk, painting, playing the piano, baking a loaf of bread, or doing some gardening can make a difference. Mindful engagement with something that totally absorbs our attention can be beneficial and help us experience healthier emotions. We are then more able to replace old inhibiting beliefs with new liberating ones.

As the Sufi master Hazrat Inayat Khan wrote, "If the mind becomes your obedient servant, the whole world is at your service."

I choose to stop and pay attention to my thoughts.
I am connected, whole, and balanced.

6. Making the changes we want to see in our lives

Sometimes we have periods in our lives when everything seems to run smoothly, without any apparent effort on our part. At other times life seems more of an uphill struggle, with sudden calamities upsetting the apple cart, unresolved tensions causing problems, or issues that we find unpalatable. Contradictions and change will always exist in our lives, but we tend to resist them, wanting to stay in our comfort zone. We can choose our attitude, however. The content of our minds is always under our control.

This is also the case when we do want to make changes in our lives. When we face challenges and realize that we need to change, and that we want our lives to change, then we can tap into our creative potential to help us deal with this. What we can imagine, we can create.

We can begin each day well. From the moment we wake up, we can give thanks for being alive, and for all we have in our lives that we value. We can choose not only to think positively but also to speak positively, because what we say has an effect. We want to create positive vibrations around us and attract good things into our lives. The less we talk negatively—about how stressed we are, or how miserable life is—the better we are going to feel. Rather than holding on to negative events from the past, we need to feel excited about the possibilities for the future. We can then direct our imagination to make the changes we want to bring about.

We can imagine scenarios that we love the idea of and desire to bring into being, and the more we can amplify our enthusiasm for our vision, the more we will attract good things into our lives. We need to really feel ourselves enjoying this new life if we want to create and affirm our belief that we are bringing it into being. Our minds have tremendous capacity for expansion, and what we choose to believe and feel is what our lives will become. Opportunities abound, and the more we can open our eyes and get excited about all the possibilities, whether people we will meet, or situations and circumstances that our positive outlook will attract, the greater will be the joy we experience.

The legendary Taoist sage, Lao Tzu, put it succinctly: "When you realize there is nothing lacking, the whole world belongs to you."

What I imagine I can create.

I choose to create positive vibrations.

I am attracting good things into my life.

7. Acting "as if"

Although our hearts may be breaking, and we may have a sense of hopelessness about our situation, if we can just stop for a moment and be still and try to focus on our breathing, we may be able to access the Source of strength inside ourselves. It's always there; it's just that we're not always connected. It's like being unplugged from an electrical outlet.

When we create a little space for ourselves amidst our suffering, we can tell ourselves that we won't be numb to the pain we feel, but that we want it to leave. Indeed, we can affirm that we "know" it is gradually leaving us. Then we might just be able to list what there is in our lives to be positive about, and to appreciate. There may well be more than we might have imagined. We can focus on those good things and give thanks, and every time we feel grateful, we feel a little better.

When we're acting "as if" we're endeavoring to contact a deep well of joy. It's worth making the effort because it has a huge impact on how we feel. It's the "smile" rather than the "stiff upper lip" approach. If we hold a particular facial expression for as little as ten seconds, it's apparently long enough to make us feel happier. When we smile, and are cheerful, people want to be around us. In the words of the popular

Louis Armstrong song, "When you're smiling, the whole world smiles with you . . ."

Similarly, if we try to act as if we're not afraid, the fear will lessen. The great novelist, academic, and poet C. S. Lewis suggested that if you don't feel love for another person, but act as if you do, the emotion will often follow the behavior. When we act as if we love someone, we do come to love them.

This is not a superficial technique, nor is it Pollyannaish in any sense. It is a means of breaking the repetitive cycle of negative thoughts and patterns of behavior. We can break free from our limited way of being into something more magnificent. We're available and receptive to what's around us, and life then responds to us with all manner of gifts.

I choose to act as if all is well.
I am available and receptive to life's magnificence.

8. Maximizing luck

No one is born lucky, for luck is something we create ourselves. True, some people may appear to be born with certain advantages, but it does not necessarily follow that they will always be lucky or that they will live full and joyous lives.

We choose how circumstances affect us—we can't control events in our lives, but we can control our reactions to them. We can also create good luck in our lives, because the opportunities are there all the time. We just need to discover, see, and act upon those opportunities. If we're trapped in negative thinking, it's not going to be possible to do this. If, however, we're relaxed, open to new experiences, prepared to take risks, and have a generally healthy and positive approach to life, we're far more likely to be lucky. We don't feel ourselves to be victims of circumstances, but instead we try to make the best of everything, working at our relationships, putting energy into our careers and interests, and getting involved in our communities.

We maximize the opportunities that come our way by trusting our intuition and making the right decisions. We're also more inclined to have positive expectations about the future. We believe our dreams will come to fruition rather than being afraid they will turn out badly. When things go wrong, we don't give up, but persevere, trusting that there is a reason why something has happened the way it has, and that something else will emerge, and the outcome will be fine. If occasionally we have to admit defeat, we don't dwell on our misfortune, but get up and have another go, taking steps to prevent a similar misfortune occurring in the future.

I make the best of everything.

I trust my intuition and my ability to make the right decisions.

I choose to persevere, trusting in the outcome.

9. Reclaiming our power to heal our bodies

The perceptions and beliefs that we've acquired over the years are extremely powerful. Bruce Lipton, the biologist, argues that they are even more powerful than our thoughts because they permeate every cell of the body. In effect, our thoughts control our biology.

Our immune system is suppressed by chronic stress, but if we feel calm, secure, and believe things will turn out okay, our body seems to maintain itself more effectively. An optimistic outlook appears to reduce stress-induced inflammation and levels of stress hormones. Also, if we see ourselves positively, it's likely that we'll have lower cardiovascular responses to stress than those who see themselves negatively, and we may also recover faster from medical procedures such as coronary bypass surgery. We're likely to live longer, both in general and when suffering from serious diseases like cancer.

Psychoneuroimmunologists have demonstrated that we can change the limiting, self-sabotaging misperceptions that underlie our thinking and behavior. Fear, anger, and guilt can all cause disease in our bodies, but letting go of the past, practicing forgiveness, and learning to be compassionate toward ourselves enables us to create balance and harmony, resulting in a more positive future. We also know that we have the power to make more conscious choices in our daily lives.

Our bodies are continually responding to the messages of our minds, and we have to take time to listen to them. There seems to be a direct correlation between a particular ailment and the message. Who or what can't we stomach? Who is a pain in the neck to us? What are we carrying on our backs? Who is getting up our nose? We don't need to blame ourselves for a condition, but likewise we shouldn't ignore what might need to change to restore our health and balance. It may be that we need more rest, a better diet, more exercise, less stress, but it could also be that we need to quit a relationship that is no longer working, or seek a more fulfilling job. We have to take time to work out where our lives are out of balance and address the issues. By getting in touch with our breathing, and getting to see what's going on in our minds, we can focus on moving toward a more harmonious balance and healing our bodies.

I am making more conscious choices.
I listen to my body and the messages it gives me.
I let go of the past.

10. Flourishing and developing resilience

All of us want to flourish—to live a life that is meaningful and makes us happy, and to be the best we can possibly be. We can't flourish, however, if we allow the tendency to be negative to rule our lives. Many research studies confirm that most of us have a greater natural tendency toward negativity than toward positivity. What we have to learn to do is to accentuate and amplify the positive.

Negative emotions have a detrimental effect on our wellbeing. Too often we feel threatened in situations and switch into survival mode, with the brain releasing stress hormones, particularly when old memories unconsciously get stirred up. We overreact, contracting and becoming defensive, distressed, or angry. We also fret about the future, imagining things that might go wrong, even if they're unlikely to happen.

Positive emotions have a hugely beneficial effect, and our brain releases oxytocin, the "love hormone," making us feel expansive, open-hearted, and open to possibilities. Not only do we feel good, but we also become more friendly, generous, and helpful to others. We are more able to develop strategies to cope with difficult situations, to manage relationships, and to be more socially responsible. To be resilient and be able to bounce back doesn't mean that we don't experience negative emotions, but that we recognize them and can let them go.

Maureen Gaffney, Adjunct Professor of Psychology and Society at Dublin University, has spent much of her working life endeavoring to understand what enables people to be at their best, to be resilient, and to flourish. It is her belief that cultivating positive emotions helps us adapt to life's inevitable ups and downs: "Positive emotions produce well-being and flourishing by making us more competent, more knowledgeable, more effective, more socially connected and more resilient."

We can all increase our ability to flourish and be resilient by actively rebalancing the positivity and negativity in our lives. It requires discipline and practice, but we can learn to manage our emotions, to be gentle with ourselves, not to judge, and to choose to think and behave in an open-hearted and positive manner.

I choose to be open-hearted and positive.
I recognize and release negative emotions.

11. Creating a better future for all

There is significant evidence from scientists working in the consciousness field that our thoughts are capable of profoundly affecting all aspects of our lives. We can use our thoughts to create a better life or to protect ourselves from unfavorable influences. It could well be that our thoughts and intentions can also help create a better future for the world.

Lynne McTaggart, researcher and writer on medicine and health, has been working with physicists and psychologists in a web-based research project that is believed to be the largest mind-over-matter experiment ever conducted: the Intention Experiment. The aim of the project is to discover how we can collectively harness the power of intention to heal the earth. Her Intention Community enables thousands of people from ninety countries around the world to experience a global sense of unity.

Many of us feel that there has to be a better way of living. The crises that confront us collectively and the tragedies occurring on a daily basis around the world seem overwhelming, yet it's possible that they are wake-up calls for us to change our ways, and are the birth pangs of a new kind of existence.

The competitive society in which we live, where we all fend for ourselves rather than working cooperatively, has resulted in alienation. Separate from one another, and from nature, the way we live, particularly in the Western world, is dysfunctional. If, however, we can heal ourselves and heal our relationships, then we have the power to heal the planet. We have the opportunity to dedicate ourselves to issues that are bigger than our own individual concerns.

If we can imagine a world that has different values, we can create it. Those values need to cherish all forms of life as sacred, all people as equal, the generations to come as just as important as our own, and the earth herself as a living, breathing organism. We need collective awareness and action so that we can all take responsibility for the future.

We can choose to be hopeful, to believe that change is not only possible but that it is already happening. There are many signs that the shift in consciousness is already unfolding, from spiritual communities that are attracting greater numbers of people to environmental initiatives, from the Slow Movement to the sharing economy. We can also choose to use our talents to conceive of, and implement, goals and strategies to help bring about the change we want to see in our world.

I am prepared to play my part in healing the planet.
I choose to be hopeful about the future.

Chapter V

Believing in
our dreams

*If one advances confidently in the direction of his
(her) dreams, and endeavors to live the life which he
(she) has imagined, he (she) will meet with a success
unexpected in common hours.*
HENRY DAVID THOREAU

We all have a dream of how we would like our life to
unfold and to a greater or lesser extent some ambitions about what we would like to achieve, but all
too often we end up disappointed once we achieve
them. Why is this?

Our dreams need to reflect who we truly are,
and not stem from past conditioning and what our
parents wanted for us, or what our teachers or peers

influenced us to pursue. We may also find that if our dreams and ambitions mean that we sacrifice some part of ourselves in the achieving, then we end up frustrated.

However, if we procrastinate, never fulfilling any kind of dream, putting the pursuit of it off to some later date because we don't have time or we doubt our capacity, we may end up regretting that we left it too late and never even tried. Germany's most famous poet, Johann Wolfgang von Goethe, urges us to get on with realizing our dream:

> Are you in earnest? Then seize this very
>   minute.
> What you can do, or dream you can,
>   begin it.
> Boldness has genius, power, and magic in it.
> Only engage and then the mind grows
>   heated;
> begin and then the work will be completed.

For our dreams to be meaningful and lead us to that place where we experience joy, they have to come from the essence of who we are, so that naturally working to achieve them becomes our passion. Only then do we feel complete and fulfilled.

How do we discover what we truly want? We know in our hearts, not with our heads. As we develop awareness and gain self-knowledge, greater clarity comes and we have an authentic sense of what our ambition is. We feel a sense of destiny, and know that it is we alone who are responsible for making the best choices for ourselves. Courage to take risks and to use our imagination, our intuition, and our creativity begin to take hold. As we define our goals and plan how to achieve them, we're inspired and motivated, energized by the Source of life within us—that same force that the poet Dylan Thomas described as, "the force that through the green fuse drives the flower."

Believing in our dream, we focus on it and ardently work at it day after day. Discipline is vital, but so is flexibility, for there are bound to be unexpected delays and developments along the way. Undeterred, we stay true to our vision, and we cultivate the feeling of excitement of our dream being realized. All the eighty trillion cells of our bodies cooperate with us, and energy flows through us so that our world expands and the possibilities seem infinite.

1. Knowing what we want/knowing who we are

We don't always know what we really want. We may think a successful career, wealth, marriage, and children are what we desire, or we may toy with the idea of doing something in the creative field, or perhaps dedicating our life to caring for others. Have we perhaps been influenced or even coerced by our parents or teachers into doing something that is not deep down what we want for ourselves?

We are often clearer about what we don't want. I was pretty certain that I did not want a life like my mother's, with the narrow confines of her world. But other than getting myself an education and seeing the world, I had no real idea how I wanted my life to unfold until my early thirties when I discovered my own passion. I had earlier fallen in love with India and its history, art. and music, but also with its philosophies, developing an interest in yoga, meditation, and personal development. I needed to earn a living, but how could I combine this with following my deepest love? Working in publishing, I imagined publishing books on the kind of subjects I was interested in. Before long I had the most amazing opportunity to found my own imprint for a major publishing house.

As I leapt to take up the opportunity, the momentum built. All kinds of doors began to open for me. My mission statement was that I would be publishing "books that contribute toward our understanding of ourselves and our place in the universe." I had a dream, I had a clear vision that came from the deepest part of myself, the Universe responded, and it felt like my destiny. As a consequence I was able to put all my passion and energy into making it a reality.

Knowing what we truly want out of life perhaps comes after several false starts, when we have a glimpse of the joy that results from doing what our heart tells us, not what the rational part of our mind tells us we ought to do. When we have a clear sense of our authentic selves and have a dream to pursue that comes from our hearts, then the life force flows through us unimpeded, we feel energized, and our life is imbued with meaning.

I trust that my heart knows what I truly want.
I allow myself to dream.

2. Realizing our passion

Discovering and then realizing our passion is what fulfills us and makes us feel alive. Some women are fortunate in that they have a desire early on in their lives to do something that burns so brightly for them that they can do nothing but follow where their heart takes them.

Many of us find our real passion later in life, but there's much we can do before then that helps us discover it and then realize it. Above all, we need to be curious about life and open to its rich variety of possibilities. As we balance our careers, our family life, and relationships, we still need to have some space and time for what are our interests alone. It's amazing how one thing can lead to another if we keep our minds open and follow up on our intuitive hunches and chance encounters. Before long, we find something to be passionate about.

If our passion turns out to be about more than achieving something just for ourselves, some higher purpose that benefits others, we will find out how the Universe helps us. The philosopher and mystic Ralph Waldo Trine, in his inspirational classic, *In Tune with the Infinite*, wrote, "A thousand unseen hands reach down to help you to their peace-crowned heights, and all the forces of the firmament shall fortify your strength."

Certainly I know from my own experience that I could never have accomplished achieving my dream had I not received incredible help from all sorts of people, and had not some wonderful opportunities simply just fallen into my lap. I was able to publish hundreds of wonderful books on health and wellbeing, personal development, and spirituality that have had an impact for the better on many women's lives, and I am convinced that this was because my intentions were not for myself alone.

Patanjali, the Indian philosopher from around the second century BC, wrote in his *Yoga Sutras*:

> When you work only for yourself, or for your own personal gain, your mind will seldom rise above the limitations of an undeveloped personal life. But when you are inspired by some great purpose, some extraordinary project, all your thoughts break your bonds: your mind transcends limitations, your consciousness expands in every direction, and you find yourself in a new, great and wonderful world. Dormant forces, faculties and talents become alive, and you discover yourself to be a greater person by far than you ever dreamed yourself to be.

Believing in our dreams

I am open to life and all its possibilities.

I am discovering my skills and talents.

I trust that help is available for me.

3. Using imagination to create our vision

Creating a vision of how we want our lives to be is like using a map when we're traveling. We can actively use our imagination to bring more joy into our lives. As the Sufi master Pir Vilayat Khan wrote: "The future is not there waiting for us. We create it by the power of imagination."

There's a well-known story about three men working in a quarry cutting blocks of stone. A passerby asks the first man what he is doing. He replies, "I'm cutting stone." The second man answers the same question with, "I'm earning a living." The third man has a different answer to the same question, "I'm building a cathedral." This man is motivated by a vision that goes way beyond his own personal needs. He is building something of enormous importance and great beauty for his community now and for future generations.

Visualization is widely employed nowadays in many walks of life, from athletes imagining their success on the track, to sales people seeing themselves closing a deal. We can all visualize what we want to create in our lives when we have a vision of what we want to accomplish and stick with it. There are many instances of ordinary people accomplishing extraordinary things.

Eileen Caddy, the spiritual teacher, had a vision about starting a community at Findhorn in Scotland. From a caravan park on the shores of the Moray Firth, she and her husband Peter grew some exceptionally large vegetables in soil where no one thought it was possible to grow anything. People began to visit, and over time a community evolved. The Findhorn Foundation now runs an educational program and attracts thousands of visitors each year. It has also become a model for many other spiritual communities.

Martin Luther King had a dream too, which became a shared vision, and that brought about social change in America and was an inspiration for countless people all over the world. Nelson Mandela also had a dream, which he never lost sight of in spite of his long imprisonment. Ultimately, he was able to end apartheid in South Africa and become the first black president of the country. His story of struggle, resilience, and ultimate triumph remains an inspiration to us all.

I use my imagination to create the future I want.
I believe that it is possible for me to accomplish
extraordinary things.

4. Practicing creative visualization

Creative visualization is something we're actually all familiar with. We use it naturally when we're day-dreaming about something we would like to happen in the future, like imagining a forthcoming holiday, a new home, or a possible relationship. We've also experienced making ourselves afraid by imagining something negative happening, creating all kinds of possible disaster scenarios.

Some years ago I had to take myself in hand every time I spent a night alone in my home. I had experienced a burglary once before in my life, and in spite of my best intentions, I found myself going to bed and feeling fearful. I really had to be firm with myself and say that nothing was going to happen, and that this was merely my mind misbehaving. I then did some positive self-talk and surrounded myself and the house with protective white light until I was able to sleep.

Neuroscientific research has demonstrated that the adult brain is malleable, and that focused mental exercises can reshape and retrain our brains. When we imagine something, our brain becomes activated as if we're actually experiencing it, since images affect the autonomic nervous system.

We can all use our imagination as a tool to change our lives, consciously creating positive images of how we want our lives to be. Shakti Gawain, in her best-selling title *Creative Visualization*, puts it succinctly:

> Creative visualization is magic in the truest and highest meaning of the word. It involves understanding and aligning yourself with the natural principles that govern the workings of our universe, and learning to use these principles in the most conscious and creative way.

First we need to relax deeply. Although there are many different techniques we can use, there are basically two simple approaches: the receptive/passive approach, which is guidance through intuition, using words, mental images, or impressions, and allows images or impressions to bubble up; and an active approach whereby we create our vision, choosing to see or experience something we have set as a goal, and making firm what we have been imagining by the use of affirmations.

Something that worked really well for me when I was at a point in my life when I knew I needed to change things and have a different sort of life, was making a collage of pictures, cut out from magazines, of how I wanted my life to look. (Images are more powerful than words.) I also kept a dream journal of how I wanted my life to unfold. I referred to these tools regularly, and tried to feel what it was like to be doing the things I dreamed of doing, and to be with the people I wanted to be with. I can assure you—it definitely works.

As we practice, and make creative visualization part of our life, then we also find that it becomes a process of deep and meaningful growth. Ultimately, creative visualization is a state of consciousness in which we are the creators of our lives, moment by moment.

I create positive images of how I want my life to be.

I allow my intuition to guide me.

5. Making the commitment

When we're fully committed to something, we can accomplish the seemingly impossible. Saying "yes" to our dreams is the first important step, but it requires a commitment to discipline and practice to bring them into being. We have to stay the course and focus on our goal for the long term.

We may discover that we hold ourselves back from achieving fulfilment in life because of negative beliefs. "I couldn't possibly do that," we might say, "I'm not clever enough," or, "I don't have the talent," but once we see these anxieties spring from past conditioning and understand how they have come about, we can create new and positive beliefs and move forward.

Whilst not wavering from our goal, we need to be gentle with ourselves, and flexible too. There's no need to be down-hearted if progress is slow, or to be put off by what others think of our efforts. Rather, we should congratulate ourselves on what we've accomplished so far. If we hit a problem, we don't give up. We keep on going, trusting that we will find a creative solution by working at it. We never know what's around the corner and how our efforts are likely to be rewarded by unexpected help.

Believing in our dreams

Johann Wolfgang von Goethe's famous and often quoted lines remind us of the importance of commitment:

Until one is committed
there is hesitancy, the chance to draw back,
always ineffectiveness.
Concerning all acts of initiative (and creation)
there is one elementary truth
the ignorance of which kills countless ideas
and splendid plans:
That the moment one definitely commits oneself
then Providence moves too.
All sorts of things occur to help one
That would never otherwise have occurred.

I commit to making my dreams reality.

I trust that help and guidance will be there when I need it.

I'm grateful for what I've been able to accomplish so far.

6. Awakening our intuitive abilities

We've all had some experience of intuition, that sense of "knowing" something without actually understanding how we know. We "feel it in our bones," we "have a hunch," a premonition, or we "pick up a vibe." Some have more developed intuitive abilities than others, but we can all access the power of intuition and develop a greater capacity to use it in our lives.

Intuition arises from a deeper level than our conscious mind. Although we tend to value rational, deductive thinking over intuition, often it's intuition that provides us with an answer when we're wondering what to do about something. Messages and guidance are coming to us all the time from what we call by various names: the Collective Unconscious, the zero-energy field, the Superconscious, God, the Source. And although we can't fathom the mystery of this, what we can do is connect with it.

We can best improve and enhance our intuitive powers by actually doing nothing at all. We can turn off our phones and laptops, forget distractions like YouTube or the TV, and just stare out of the window. We can watch the clouds, or notice the shapes of trees, or gaze at the waves hitting the shoreline, or the eddies in a fast-flowing river. We can look really closely at people who are passing by, and we can listen for the sounds of birdsong, snatches of conversation, or the lines of a song. It's surprising what comes to us when we're relaxed but alert, and how something may seem of significance.

Awakening intuition and developing awareness go together. When we quiet down the mind and learn to focus our attention, we begin to see that we have more possibilities and more choices in our lives. As we learn to trust our intuition, we find that we are able to create the future we want through the choices we make.

❦

I choose to connect with the Source of life.

I allow my intuition to bubble up.

I trust my intuition to help me make the right choices.

7. Using dreams to bring us closer to our goal

Dreams and intuition are linked, and we can all learn to use our dreams as a source of guidance. Dreams also help develop intuition, for as we learn more about ourselves through dreams, we naturally become more intuitive.

Throughout history, dreams have been regarded as significant. In ancient Greece the sanctuaries of Asclepius, the god of healing, were widespread, and people went to them to receive a healing dream from the god. In traditional shamanic cultures, found amongst the Native Americans, the Aborigines of Australia, some of the tribes of Africa, the indigenous peoples of South America, and many Siberian tribes, the shamans are healers and work with dreams to help treat illness. The Senoi people of Malaysia use dreams on a daily basis for guidance, and children are taught to share their dreams each morning and to control dreams through lucid dreaming.

Clearly, dreams are of far more significance than we tend to believe. Many people say that they don't dream, meaning, however, that they are not in touch with their dreams.

Freud called dreams, "the royal road to the unconscious," and Jung believed dreams revealed psychological truths. Artists, writers, and even scientists have found them to be a source of inspiration. Einstein, for example, got many of his best ideas when he was in a relaxed and drowsy state in front of the fire, brandy glass in hand. August Kekule discovered the benzene ring after seeing an image of a snake biting its tail in a dream. Henri Poincaré, the French mathematician, certainly believed in the power of dreams and intuition, writing, "It is by logic that we prove. It is by intuition that we discover."

Dreams are a powerful source of information about our subconscious mind and how we feel. They often reflect what has happened, is happening, or may happen in the future. We need to pay attention to our dreams and develop our awareness of them, along with developing our intuitive abilities. We can reflect and prepare for dreams each night by asking for guidance with a problem we want to solve. It's a good idea to keep a notebook by the bed, and program ourselves to wake slowly, making a note of any dream or part of a dream we remember on waking.

I pay attention to my dreams.
I trust my dreams to give me insight.
I can ask for guidance.

8. Unlocking our creativity

Creativity is a natural ability we all possess. It's not something exclusive to artists, musicians, or writers, since we all have imagination and can use it to create something. We just need to allow ourselves time and space to experiment with making choices, shaping things, and giving substance to our dreams. Each of us is unique and has something to offer that is uniquely ours.

We need courage to risk being creative, and inspiration to motivate us, but above all else we need to follow our hearts and do what we love to do most. "If genius is anything," writes the remarkable choreographer Twyla Tharp in *The Creative Habit*, "it is that love for what you do that is so great that working tirelessly to be better at it is not *work* in the way we commonly think of work but more like play."

Creating anything, whether it's a loaf of bread, an arrangement of flowers in a vase, or a painting or sculpture, can be deeply satisfying. When we forget about ourselves because we're so totally absorbed in a creative activity, we leave our egos behind and become attuned to the natural creative flow of the Universe.

At the end of his life, the poet and novelist D. H. Lawrence maintained that the process of creativity is essentially a religious activity because it connects us to what is greater than ourselves. When we can unlock our creativity by throwing ourselves into what we love to do, and letting go of any doubts about our ability, and any fears of being criticized or ridiculed, when we are at one with the process of creation, joy is what we find.

I allow myself the space and time to be creative.
I follow my heart in letting my creativity unfold.
I connect with the Source of life.

9. Underpinning with discipline

If we want to realize our dreams, we have to underpin our creativity and imagination with discipline. Routine is essential, as is total discipline. We can't necessarily sit and wait for inspiration—we have to make a start, as the French sculptor Auguste Rodin advised:

Where shall we begin?
    There is no beginning. Start where you arrive. Stop before what entices you. And work! You will enter little by little into the entirety. Method will be born in proportion to your interest.
    In the calm exile of work, we must learn patience, which in turn teaches energy, and

energy gives us eternal youth made of self-collectedness and enthusiasm.

Inspiration may be slow to begin with, but if we apply ourselves, it often follows. We have to set a schedule and then stick to it. Commitment to that schedule day after day becomes a habit, and we find it has its own rhythm. The love for what we are doing brings with it energy and dedication. Many of the world's greatest artists and writers follow a consistent, disciplined schedule. We shouldn't let hesitancy and self-doubt put us off—we need to silence that inner critic who tells us we can't do it, probably based on some past memory of being told we're lacking in creative skills. We don't procrastinate or make excuses; instead we have to make room for our creative work every day. We set goals, work toward them, and eliminate distractions, while at the same time getting on with what has to be done in our lives to keep body and soul together.

Discipline helps us order the chaos that somehow seems prerequisite for the birth of anything worthwhile. This book began as a series of folders stuffed full of half-written pieces and thoughts on my themes. I wrote notes to myself, questions about whether subsections might be better elsewhere, ideas to follow up on, gaps to be filled, or a particular quotation to be found. As the weeks went by, the chaos gradually gave way to order as I disciplined myself to working consistently on the project.

We may have days when we don't seem to achieve much, or are not happy with what we've done. But we hone our skills, keep at it, and avoid making negative judgments. We need to be gentle with ourselves. If it's temporarily not going well, then we can pause, focus on our breathing, and accept that we are where we are at this very moment in time. Then we can take a short break to do something nurturing like going for a walk or listening to some music. I tend to go out in the garden and pull a few weeds or do some dead-heading and generally forget about what the problem was. Then we return to the task in hand, with gratitude for the life we have and the progress we're making on our project. Hard work and patience reap rewards—we become absorbed in what we're doing and feel alive, finding our inner source of joy.

I commit to being disciplined in my creative efforts.
I trust that I can create something worthwhile.
I am patient.

10. Going with the flow and releasing attachment

Once we're reconnected to the Source of the natural creative energy that flows through us, we are powerful, and can achieve what it is we truly desire. We see things differently and are able to open fully to life and participate more. An expanded state of consciousness makes us feel in love with life and new options and possibilities. We make different choices—we meet new people, try out different places, become interested in things that didn't appeal to us before, and we find our circle of acquaintances widens. We no longer need to struggle to control our lives, we can relax and let go. We feel we can tackle whatever lies ahead. We also find that the more we interact with others and focus less on our own concerns, the more joyful our lives become.

This is the opposite of what happens when we're stressed and in crisis mode, when we tend to shut down and become contracted. Life no longer feels exciting because we've become disconnected from the Source of joy in our lives. Not that a crisis is totally without benefits—often it is a catalyst for change. Difficult and challenging times can be an opportunity to take stock and review our hopes and dreams.

Once we've found our true passion and are engaged in doing everything we can to fulfill it, it's also important to be willing to accept and release what the end result may be. Attachment can turn to obsession, and then we are less likely to be able to make our dream a reality. We need to release our attachment to the outcome, because we cannot make it happen. We don't have total control, so we have to be flexible, and we have to go with the flow.

I can relax knowing that I'm connected to the flow of life.

I accept that I don't have total control.

I am flexible and go with the flow.

Chapter VI

Practicing kindness

If I can stop one heart from breaking,
I shall not live in vain;
If I can ease one life the aching,
Or cool one pain,
Or help one fainting robin
Unto his rest again,
I shall not live in vain.

EMILY DICKINSON

Practicing kindness can transform our lives as well as affecting those around us. It can also be beneficial to extend kindness even to people we don't know.

We live in a culture that fails to appreciate that we're all connected. We see ourselves as separate from the Source of life and from each other. Our self-absorption and our tendency to want to look out for our own interests have resulted in conflict and domination, rather than harmony and cooperation.

If, instead, we could begin to recognize our shared humanity and the deep connection we all share, as different cultures in the past once did, and as indigenous societies today still do, and if we could extend that sense of connection to include all life forms and the generations to come, then it's possible we would not be experiencing so many of the crises that we are witnessing in our world today.

All the great humanitarians and teachers of different religious traditions have stressed the importance of kindness, love, and compassion. The so-called Golden Rule of treating others as we would wish ourselves to be treated runs through all religions. "My religion is kindness," says the Dalai Lama. The Talmud, the Jewish book of wisdom, claims, "The highest wisdom is kindness." Jesus told us to "love one another as I have loved you." The Koran asks, "Do you love your Creator? Then love your fellow beings first." The perceptive writer Aldous Huxley, having explored mysticism and altered states of consciousness, said on his deathbed, "Let us be kinder to one another."

Kindness radiates from the joy we naturally experience when we are connected to the Source of all life—the Self, the life force, chi, God, Brahman, the zero-energy field—whatever it is we want to call it. We can however develop the trait of kindness through the practice of loving kindness meditation. Research has shown that whatever positive and loving feelings are generated whilst practicing, they are likely to imbue the rest of the day with positivity and kindness. Loving kindness meditation makes us more open and more likely to be optimistic when a situation is challenging, and we are likely to improve the quality of our relationships.

First we practice being gentle toward ourselves, opening our hearts and extending feelings of warmth, love, and kindness. We need to do more than just think about this. We need to really evoke the warm and loving feelings so that we feel we're glowing with love. Sometimes, if this feels difficult, we just need to accept what comes up. We can help the process by imagining what it feels like to hold a newborn baby, or touch the soft coat of a kitten, or smell the perfume of a rose. Once we've successfully managed to feel that softness and warmth, we can then try expanding this outward to others—our partners, parents, children, friends, neighbors, acquaintances, and so on, until we are able to extend it to the entire world. Such a practice, when done regularly, begins to help change the way we relate and behave in our lives.

Cognitive scientists have demonstrated that being kind and helping others gives a greater sense of wellbeing than gratifying our personal desires. Kindness produces measurable physiological changes in the body—our oxytocin levels rise and the heart rate goes down from the baseline level, lowering cortisol, so we are definitely in a relaxed state. We feel happier and our health also benefits.

Acts of kindness strengthen relationships and communities, since there are domino effects, with a single kind act cascading down to many more people than we can imagine. Paying compliments, if genuine, is also another way of brightening someone's day. Kindness is also good in work environments and in business—productivity and sales can improve when employees and customers are treated well, and colleagues who are kinder to each other feel happier in their work as a result.

Mother Teresa, the epitome of kindness, wrote:

Spread love everywhere you go: first of all in your own homes. Give love to your children, to your wife or husband, to a next door neighbor . . . Let no one ever come to you without leaving better and happier. Be the living expression of God's kindness; kindness in your face, kindness in your eyes, kindness in your smile, kindness in your warm greeting.

1. Being gentle with ourselves

The relationship we have with ourselves is the starting point for the relationship we have with others and practicing kindness toward them. As women, we often put other people's needs before our own. This is not necessarily altruistic on our part, since we may well be meeting other people's needs in order to get our own needs met. Giving our time and energy is fine if we have it to give, and we don't in any sense feel diminished by giving, but first we need to nurture and be kind to ourselves.

When we're gentle with ourselves, we're honoring our true selves, not the self-image we've created of ourselves. We don't need to strive for approval, or to blame and criticize, or be hard on ourselves for something we think we should have done. We just need to soften and listen to what our intuition is telling us we need at this moment in time.

When we experience disappointment, loss, or pain, instead of closing down and tensing up, we can try to remain open, so that we can see other possibilities and choices that might be available to us. Instead of trying to protect ourselves by suppressing or trying to stop the painful feelings, or by reacting and retaliating, we need to acknowledge the feelings we're experiencing, without judging them, and recognize that they are just feelings.

There may well be occasions when we feel alone and powerless, and sometimes it's difficult to accept a situation, or it's necessary for us to grieve. Whatever the circumstances, we need to be kind to ourselves and recognize that we are doing the best we can at this moment in time. Giving ourselves the space to be present in our bodies, we can use conscious breathing to allow the mind to become still. As the feelings arise, we can accept them and let them go. It may help to take a walk, indulge in a warm, scented bath, sit in the sun, play some music, or give ourselves a hug and tell ourselves how wonderful we are. As we begin to feel more connected to the life force that flows through us, we can relax and release, and feel more at ease. One of my favorite phrases to repeat as a mantra is "relax, release, return to Source." If I say this a few times, I find my shoulders dropping, my breath slowing, and a sense of connection returning. There's nothing self-indulgent or narcissistic about being kind to ourselves—it's prerequisite for being genuinely kind to others.

I love and honor my true self.
I trust that I am doing the best I can.
I relax, release, and return to Source.

2. Opening our hearts and making kindness a habit

Once we're able to be kind to ourselves and take care of what we really need without looking to someone else to provide it, we find ourselves more naturally openhearted. Maintaining this open heart is the key to warm, nurturing relationships with others, whoever they are.

It's easy to be open-hearted when things are going well in our lives, but we find it much more difficult if we're contracted because we're sad, or depressed, or resentful. This is why it's so essential to cultivate the habit of kindness. A regular "self-compassion practice" helps establish a pattern of practicing kindness toward ourselves, and once we're feeling at ease, we can more easily appreciate the bond between ourselves and others. When we know how interconnected we all are, we are more able to open our hearts to others.

We can practice being warm, gentle, and kind to all the people we meet in the course of our daily activities, offering welcoming words, caring gestures, and support when needed. We can pay attention, listen closely to what they say, appreciate their unique qualities and talents, and increase our sense of connection with them.

Kindness is really an expression of love. Dr. Barbara Fredrickson, Professor of Psychology at the University of North Carolina at Chapel Hill, has spent many years researching positive emotions, which she advocates cultivating by using loving kindness meditation so that we can experience "micro-moments" of positive resonance and connection with everyone we encounter. Her research demonstrates that when we're kind to others we're all healthier, happier, and inclined to live longer.

I feel at ease with myself.
I practice kindness throughout the day wherever
     I can.
I open my heart to all.

3. Nurturing our most intimate relationships

Intimacy is good for us. Medical research has shown that where there is affection, empathy, and support, intimate relationships promote health and longevity. Our ideas about intimacy have changed over time, shaped by economic, social, and cultural conditions. In today's world there's a tendency to think intimacy is only something we have with our immediate partners. We can, however, have an intimate relationship with our parents, children, grandchildren, or friends.

Intimacy requires us to be open, to pay attention, and above all to be kind to one another. Through constant, mindful practice of being more loving, we deepen our connection with others as our relationships constantly improve and as we feel happier and enriched ourselves, not least because feeling connected releases endorphins.

If we're too busy and preoccupied with our own concerns, we're not able to give sufficient time to important others in our lives. We cannot put our own pleasure first if we want to have a truly intimate and loving relationship. We need to be there for the other person, maybe at a time not convenient for us. Giving someone time requires giving of ourselves fully—it's an expression of our love for them, and that love has to be given without wanting anything in return.

We also need to allow for the differences that exist in each other, and not expect the other person necessarily to fulfill our needs and expectations. We need to let go of wanting love or approval. That is why it's so important to be at ease with who we are. There does need to be mutuality so that we respect and honor each other for who we each are, and both reach out, listen, and encourage one another. Above all we need to make a committed decision to be kind, however we may feel and whatever the situation, aiming to help each other on our own particular journey.

Kindness and appreciation flow back and forth in an intimate relationship like the ebb and flow of the tide. Genuine feelings of love and appreciation arise when we recognize that someone goes out of their way to do something that they know will make us happy. When we appreciate their kindness, and tell them how much we appreciate it, they feel good. Our relationship is therefore strengthened by these mutual positive feelings.

I commit to being more loving.

I respect difference.

I choose to be kind without wanting anything in return.

4. Having realistic expectations of others

If we want to experience greater love and joy in our lives, taking responsibility for our own wellbeing and not expecting someone else to make us happy is crucial. It's no good bringing those emotional needs from our childhood into our relationships and expecting them to disappear automatically. Not that we do that consciously, but certainly our fears and insecurities stemming from the experiences of our early lives undoubtedly rear their heads in our intimate relationships. Neither does it help if we're unable to talk about what we want in a relationship and expect the other party to be a mind reader. We have to have clarity about our wishes and be able to express them.

Having realistic expectations of the other person is vital. We have to be aware enough to have some understanding of their nature. And we have to allow them to be themselves, we can't try to control them or attempt to make them into someone they're not. Often our love is conditional—we do not accept them as they are. They cannot, however, be the ideal we might like them to be, fulfilling our needs. We have to accept that they have their faults and imperfections, as do we, as well as the qualities we admire.

We need to be courageous and open enough to learn about the other and what makes them tick. When we love another person, it is their happiness and wellbeing that is paramount, not ours. This doesn't mean that we ignore our desires and needs, but we have to be realistic about them and where they're coming from, and whether the relationship can provide what it is we're looking for, or whether there is another way to find fulfillment.

If we seek to be loved and expect to be loved, we will be disappointed. Rather we have to make the decision and commitment to be kind in all circumstances, with no guarantee of being loved in return. Love, however, flows when we're loving human beings and show genuine kindness as much as we possibly can.

I communicate my needs with clarity.

I allow _____ to be themselves.

I am kind in all circumstances.

5. Listening and communicating with kindness

Relating requires that we genuinely listen to people and communicate with kindness. Listening is an art, almost a mindfulness practice in itself. Too often we're poor listeners, reluctant to give our full attention. We're preoccupied with our own thoughts, or we feel we haven't the time to engage in conversation, and must get on with the next thing on our to-do list. Or, if we're half-listening to the person speaking, we're already thinking about our response, or we interrupt rather than let them finish what they're saying. We're so self-absorbed generally that we deprive ourselves of the opportunity of experiencing those micro-moments of connection.

Sometimes we agree with the person talking because we want to be liked and don't want to get into an argument, but whether in our interpersonal relationships at home or in the workplace, it's important to speak, although mindful of respecting the other person, in a manner that reflects how we feel. If we withhold our truth we're not being our authentic self, and as a result we are likely to feel resentful.

When we speak, it's not just our words that matter, but also our tone of voice, our facial expressions, and our body language. We need to choose our words consciously, aware of our eye contact and our gestures. Essentially we need to slow down and speak from our feelings. To do this we have to be comfortable with silence too, which is an integral part of the rhythm of conversation. If we give our full attention to listening and pause before replying, we are more likely to be in tune with both the spoken and the unspoken messages being communicated.

I listen to _____ with my full attention.

I have the courage to express my feelings.

I pay attention both to what I say and how I say it.

6. Appreciating our parents

Some women are fortunate to have a close and loving relationship with their parents for much of their lives, even as they age and roles tend to become reversed. Many of us, however, struggle to some degree with our parental relationships. Sooner or later we need to be kinder to our parents, or even to their memory.

First of all, it's worth remembering that without them we would not be here. They took care of us as best they could, even if that care was not always wise and loving. If abuse was an issue, it is likely that their own parents abused them. We need to try to understand why they acted as they did.

Unfortunately, even the best parenting is flawed. We are all human and so there are likely to have been times when our parents would not have dealt with us skillfully, just as we do not always behave well. The hurts and disappointments we might have felt in our childhood remain with us. Coming to terms with this and understanding and practicing forgiveness, is the only way through if we are to leave those hurts and disappointments behind and mature as human beings.

My own relationship with my mother was often prickly. Having had me at a young age, it was only later in life that she admitted that she felt a degree of resentment about the freedom and opportunities that I enjoyed in my life that she felt were not available to her. At the same time, I gradually came to realize that much of the difficulty I experienced when we spent any time together was that I wanted her to be someone other than who she was. Because of her lack of education I felt unable to share to any extent my interests or my hopes and dreams. As the years passed, there was more of a mutual respect in our relationship. Although there was much about me that my mother was unable or unwilling to understand, she became proud of me and what I had achieved in my life. Likewise, I came to admire and love the woman who was widowed at thirty-five, who lost my sister and her great grand-daughter before her own death at the age of eighty-four, and yet in spite of this had been strong, able, and fiercely independent. She had done the very best that she could possibly have done for me in the circumstances in which we found ourselves, and more besides—she had helped me grow.

I feel love and gratitude toward my parents, knowing that they do or did their best for me.

I accept my parents for who they are or were.

7. Giving of ourselves as mothers

Loving our own children and caring for them can test our ability to be kind to the limit. It means having endless patience and the capacity for self-sacrifice. A new baby is all-consuming in terms of its needs, utterly dependent on its mother. Baby and mother are absorbed in each other, but however thrilled we are with our little bundles of joy, when the baby screams and writhes, it's a challenge initially to know what it wants. Life becomes an endless round of feeding, changing, washing, and amusing. As new mothers know (and nowadays new fathers, too), it's exhausting, and with sleep patterns disrupted we women seem to be permanently tired, have no time for ourselves, probably don't feel that we look our best, and are suffering from "baby brain."

Neither does it seem to get easier. Once the baby is crawling, mothers need eyes like hawks, anticipating falls and head-bangs on sharp-ended furniture. There are messy mealtimes as a child learns to eat, while the paraphernalia of childhood in the form of toys and learning aids take over the living room.

When the second child comes along, even with a partner who shares the tasks, and help from willing grandparents, life is no longer our own. Previous interests are put on hold, and instead we want to make the world a better place for our offspring, making sure they have all the right opportunities. The world now revolves around our progeny. If we return to work, even if part-time, there are so many balls to juggle. Making sure we pull our weight in the office even though we may need to take time out because our child is sick, finding a day care, worrying about future schooling, stretching the finances, maintaining an intimate relationship with our partner . . . there are times when it all seems so completely overwhelming.

Although it may become easier as children grow older, there are always challenges, and care and attention are still necessary. Being a skillful parent means being loving at all times, instilling discipline gently but firmly, encouraging and being supportive, as well as imparting core values that will help our children flourish throughout their lives.

Even though we want the best for our children, we also have to guard against trying to live their lives for them. We need to let them make their own choices and their own mistakes. Aggressive parenting turns children into achievement machines, groomed from birth to be successful, according to their parents' wishes, not their own. It also produces children unable to stand on their own two feet because they are so used to being helped by their parents. Children need to be given a certain amount of free rein to follow their dreams—they don't need us trying to orchestrate every aspect of their lives.

Having children is a great way to learn that we are not the center of the Universe. There is undoubtedly something very precious about family life, but the lessons we all learn about ourselves is probably the most important thing of all.

I choose to be loving at all times.

I allow my children to make their own choices.

I am not the center of the Universe.

8. Deepening our friendships

When we are with good friends, kindness comes spontaneously. The connections and threads that tie our lives together, the shared rituals and experiences, the laughter and fun we enjoy, and the support and encouragement when it's needed, mean a great deal to us. It's natural for us to be kind to one another, taking the time to remember birthdays or to be in touch before an important event, sending thank-you notes, and offering help when needed. The relationship with our good friends is intimate, easy, with rarely any friction, though we may not agree on everything. We appreciate having such friends in our lives and are happy to go to great lengths to maintain and nurture these friendships. Research shows that feeling connected releases endorphins so there's no doubt that friendship is good for our health—as if we didn't know!

Several times a year I meet up with a circle of close girlfriends. We have been friends for many years now and shared careers and holidays together, experienced individually and collectively widowhood, divorce, singledom, new partners, aging parents, children, and grandchildren. The bond we share feels special, and whenever we meet up, there's never enough time and, like all good friends, we vow we must meet up again soon. To spend time together is positively uplifting—we laugh a lot, we confide any worries, and we share our hopes and dreams for the future. Joy overflows and is as efficacious as champagne. We appreciate how lucky we are and what a great thing friendship is.

I also have another group of friends with whom I share a different bond, more of a spiritual friendship. What ties us together is our common purpose of long-term practicing of Indian singing. We do not have intertwined lives, we are all very different (different ages, different sexes, different languages, different cultures, different religions, different political persuasions, and differences in our economic means), so much so that it's not always a comfortable relationship, though we are respectful of the differences between us. Yet, this group of friends is important. Because we're not alike and are lives are so different, we have to make more effort, and we learn things about ourselves; we get to see what creatures of habit we are, and how our likes and dislikes are a reflection of how strong our ego is. Our friendship, however, gives us an opportunity to practice loving kindness. Our teacher's patient and loving guidance, the singing together that we enjoy so much, and the support we give each other, makes us appreciate the deep connection that we share.

I appreciate and nurture my friendships.
I am respectful of difference.
I practice loving kindness as much as I can.

9. The healing balm of kindness

Many years ago now, after a period of being single following the end of my marriage, I made the decision that the most important quality I wanted in any future partner was kindness. This was different from what I had previously thought important, and was a reflection of some measure of maturity after what I had been through.

One day when my new partner and I were renovating the house, a raku vase that I particularly loved and that stood on the landing was caught by the new blinds the handyman was about to install, with the result that it crashed to the ground. It had been a present from my ex-husband. It was exquisitely beautiful and I had always felt that it had magical properties because of its vaguely esoteric design and brilliant colors.

I was upset when I saw the mass of tiny pieces on the ground. I interpreted it as a sign that all connection with my ex-husband, including any residual pain, was now well and truly over. Later on I wondered whether I could have used insurance money to get a new one made by the same potter as a symbol of a new life. I managed to track him down, only to find that he now no longer lived in the country and was also no longer working in that medium. *An interesting message from the Universe*, I thought, smiling to myself.

However, knowing how much the vase had meant to me, my new partner took the pieces that he had swept up and saved. He sat down, and taking glue, wire, and a huge amount of patience, he reassembled it piece by piece. The vase is not what it was before—it's full of cracks like crazy paving, but it means more to me now than it ever did. In Japan, a fractured item is seen as an opportunity to create a new one. Broken ceramics are stuck back together and the cracks are emphasized with silver and gold, making the item even more valuable.

A special vase can be made whole again, and a broken heart can be healed. For me this experience was a wonderful lesson in the power of kindness as love in action.

I open myself to receive the healing balm of kindness.
I practice kindness, for it is love in action.

10. Understanding those who cause us pain

Practicing kindness in all circumstances is challenging enough even with our loved ones. But what about those who've wronged us in some way? How do we manage to practice kindness toward them? The answer is that it takes time, but above all, understanding. Baruch Spinoza, the philosopher, wrote: "Do not weep; do not wax indignant. Understand."

Endeavoring to cultivate positive emotions is always more beneficial for us than perpetuating never-ending cycles of anger and hatred. Both victim and perpetrator suffer when wrong is done, but revenge is never sweet because it only gives momentary gratification. We need to stop being self-absorbed and try putting ourselves in the other person's shoes in order to understand.

We can begin with a little self-compassion practice for ourselves. When we feel loving kindness toward ourselves, we recognize our own anger, fear, greed, or shame. We have to open our hearts and see that we all have to combat these negative feelings. We are then more easily able to accept negative feelings in others and feel empathy for them. As the poet Henry Wadsworth Longfellow reminded us: "If we could read the secret history of our enemies, we would find in each man's life a sorrow and a suffering enough to disarm all hostility."

Those who have hurt us may be one thing, but what about the terrible things that happen in our world on a daily basis, past or present—murder, rape, exploitation, torture, abuse, and the violent insanities of war and terrorism? How are we to feel toward the perpetrators? Instead of making judgments and condemning, we need to try to understand. That's not to excuse or condone what has been done or to suggest that they shouldn't be punished if they've committed heinous crimes, but, as the Buddha said: "Never in the world does hatred cease by hatred; hatred ceases by love."

I put myself in the other person's shoes.

I open my heart and recognize that we all experience suffering.

I try to understand rather than judge.

11. Widening the circle of
our kindness

In the past the idea that we were all mutually interdependent was more obvious than it is today—people
knew their neighbors and the local shopkeepers and
tradespeople. Nowadays we tend to see ourselves as
separate individuals and are more preoccupied with
our own interests than ever before. We may be connected digitally, and there is greater awareness of
what is going on around the world, but there is also
far more loneliness, alienation, and depression.

We're making a mistake when we fail to see ourselves as interconnected and interdependent. As the
great physicist and philosopher Albert Einstein said
in a passage often quoted:

> A human being is a part of the whole called
> by us "the universe," a part limited in time and
> space. He experiences himself, his thoughts and
> feelings, as something separate from the rest—a
> kind of optical delusion of consciousness. This
> delusion is a kind of prison for us, restricting
> us to our personal desires and affection for a
> few persons nearest to us. Our task must be to
> free ourselves from this prison by widening the
> circle of our understanding and compassion to

embrace all living creatures and the whole of nature in its beauty.

We don't want to feel vulnerable, and yet the acceptance of our vulnerability is prerequisite for extending kindness. We need to be open and flexible to deepen our sense of connection to others. We are, after all, in the same boat, all wanting the same thing from life—happiness and the avoidance of suffering.

Being kind has been shown to improve our happiness and our health. Martin Seligman, the pioneer of the positive psychology movement, found in his research experiments that performing an act of kindness was far more likely to generate a sense of well-being than just having enjoyable experiences.

We tend to be kind automatically to our family and friends, but find it more difficult to help, for example, the homeless, those in prison, or immigrants. We may well make charitable donations, but we feel uneasy about getting physically involved, and we may feel guilty about not doing more if we ourselves are in a comfortable situation.

The answer is that we need to do what we can, whilst at the same time increasing our sense of connection with them, which means accepting them as they are. We can work on extending our kindness through practices like loving kindness meditation, beginning with ourselves and opening our eyes, minds, and hearts to seeing others more fully, and encouraging warm and tender feelings to arise as we wish them well, gradually extending out beyond those we know to all beings. One of the most popular texts of Buddhism is the *Maitri Sutra*, the sutra on kindness, from which these lines come:

> May all beings be happy and at their ease! May they be joyous and live in safety! All beings whether weak or strong, in high, middle or low realms of existence, small or great, visible or invisible, near or far away, born or to be born— may all beings be happy and at their ease! . . . So with a boundless mind should one cherish all living beings, radiating friendliness over the entire world, above, below, and all around without limit.

I choose to deepen my sense of connection with others.
I extend kindness to all beings.

Trusting life's process

Everything that happens to you is your teacher. The secret is to learn to sit at the feet of your own life and be taught by it.
Everything that happens is either a blessing which is also a lesson, or a lesson which is also a blessing.
POLLY BERRIEN BERENDS

Poets, philosophers, and mystics of many persuasions have viewed the world as a school, where we come as souls to learn.

Although we may find the idea of reincarnating over many lifetimes difficult to take on board, we can see that even in a single lifespan we have many experiences and are constantly learning and changing as a result of them. As the writer Virginia Woolf wrote, "A self that goes on changing is a self that goes on living." We have to change or life isn't really lived, and events constantly force us to change and to grow as human beings. For the poet John Keats, who wrote movingly about life being a school where souls come to learn, it's "a world of circumstances" that our heart responds to that makes us who we are. For Emmanuel, the spirit channeled by Pat Rodegast, it's the limitations that we see existing in our world that provide us with the opportunity to learn who we truly are: "If this world were a perfect place, where would souls go to school?"

We need to trust life and the process of its unfolding, and we need to keep our hearts open. We cannot be so fearful that we spend our time trying to protect ourselves, or so closed down that we cannot receive what the Universe has to give us. We know that physiologically a heart that is closed down with negative emotions will not function well, and conversely that when the heart overflows with love and warmth, not only do we feel amazing, but also that it's better for our health and longevity.

When we are able to be at ease with ourselves, we trust ourselves and are more able to trust others, and when we trust life, then we experience moments of grace. Grace is constantly available to us. The first snowdrops in winter, the scent of spring blossoms carried on the breeze, sand under our bare feet, the smile of a baby, or the choir singing in the church as we pass by—all that delights and lifts the spirits is a form of grace. It is also grace that enables us to cope with life's curveballs and find the strength we need—in the form of an unexpected offer of help, a sudden insight, or a phone call from a much-loved friend. And it is grace that enables us to experience that there is more to life than we could ever possibly have imagined.

1. Keeping our hearts open

For the Ancient Egyptians the heart was the center of thought, memory, and emotion. It was believed to hold the account of how a life had been lived. When someone died, there was the symbolic Weighing of the Heart Ceremony, described in the text known as *The Book of the Dead*. The heart was weighed on a pair of scales against the principle of truth and justice, represented by a feather. If the heart balanced against the feather, then the deceased was granted a place in the afterlife. If it weighed heavy with wrongdoings, a terrifying beast devoured the heart.

For all of us, the role of the heart is crucial. In terms of our physiology, the heart beats 100,000 times a day and pumps 2,000 gallons of blood around our bodies. It sends oxygen and nutrients to every cell and carries away unwanted carbon dioxide and waste products. We know how vital it is to keep our hearts functioning well, and to that end we avoid smoking and excessive drinking, we are careful with our eating habits, and we exercise regularly.

Just as important is being mindful of our emotional health and how we manage stress. Emotions like anger, despair, and depression can be very damaging over the long term as we close down, even to the point of closing our physical bodies around the heart to try and protect it. This affects our posture and breathing and the heart begins to be unable to do its job properly. The blood flows less easily through the arteries and veins, with the inevitable disastrous consequences.

We have to stay open to life, which means keeping our hearts open and accepting and experiencing pain. We have to be willing to accept change, however uncomfortable and threatening it may feel. We have to avoid resisting and closing down. To do this means that we have to be prepared to trust what we feel deep inside, and to have faith that all will be well, whatever we're experiencing.

There are times when we are confused as we try to work something out: Why did such and such happen? Why me? Why now? We go round and round in circles endlessly, but fail to come up with an answer. It's far better to sit quietly and listen to the voice that speaks from the heart. This is the voice that resonates with the core of our being, and the one we need to learn to trust. When we are able to act from the insight that comes from that place we trust, then things tend to work out best for our growth and wellbeing.

I trust life and its process.

I trust the voice that speaks from within.

I open my heart, knowing everything is good for my growth and wellbeing.

2. Having faith in ourselves and others

Who can we trust? We certainly can't put our trust in governments and politicians, the stock markets and financiers, or any of the things that our materialistic culture deems of value like power, money, possessions, celebrity, youth, or good looks, all of which are unreliable or ephemeral. Yet trust is essential in society if it's to function well, which is why we need values of justice, fairness, and equality, with everyone's best interests at its core.

Trust is also vital in relationships, but many of us have difficulty trusting others, even if it's our family, friends, and colleagues. Again, this is hardly surprising given that we may have been let down, deceived, or sadly even abused in our lives. Learning to trust requires wisdom and experience.

Neither do we always trust ourselves. We don't trust that we are making the right choices, for we choose without necessarily knowing what will be best in the long run. We also know that we can't always trust ourselves to keep our resolutions or stick to agreements we've made with others. We don't always trust our reactions in a situation, for we do not always manage our emotions skillfully. This means that when we slip up, our self-esteem and self-respect suffer. We can, however, learn to trust our authentic selves.

The Latin word for trust, *fides*, is also the same as the word for faith. We tend to talk about being faithful and having faith in something, and we know that it gives us a sense of security. Faith in a power greater than ourselves (whether we call it Source, God, Spirit, Nature, the Universe, Brahman, or Allah doesn't matter) gives us that sense of connection and belonging. When our faith is genuine and comes from the deepest part of ourselves, and is neither something we follow blindly, nor imposed upon us from outside, we are able to trust ourselves to make the right choices and decisions. When we trust who we really are then we respect ourselves.

Learning to trust when we've been particularly unfortunate and suffered greatly can take a long time. If someone has proved untrustworthy, rather than judging and condemning them, we need to take time to reflect on the fact that there will be a reason for their behavior, which at this point in time we do not understand. There is a Native American saying that is particularly apt here: "Do not judge someone until you have walked a mile in their moccasins." Perhaps the best way of dealing with this is to recognize the Divine Spark that exists in everyone, whatever they've done. If we can respect that place of integrity and trust the essential goodness of it, we may well find that we can begin to trust others once again.

I trust myself to make the right decisions and choices.
I recognize the Divine Spark that exists in everyone,
    even those who have hurt me.

3. Accepting the seasons of our heart

We can observe the changing seasons of nature, and we can also see that there are seasons in our lives. "And you would accept the seasons of your heart, even as you have always accepted the seasons that pass over your fields," wrote Kahlil Gibran in *The Prophet*.

Although we have our dreams and plans, they don't always unfold as we want them to. One moment everything seems to be going well, then unforeseen circumstances intervene, the twists and turns of fate catch us out, and we can be so devastated by a tragic turn of events that it seems impossible that we will ever recover. Yet, we can compare the process of constant change in nature with its birth, flourishing, decay, and regeneration. The knowledge that this is how it is can help us trust the seasons of our hearts.

Spring always comes, however hard and dark the winter. Everything bursts into life with such promise, and in the halcyon days and nights of light-filled summer we celebrate the abundance of life and the glimpse of eternity. As the cycle of blossoming and harvest reaches its climax, our hearts are filled with gratitude. With the lengthening shadows and chill shorter days, autumn arrives and everything begins to die down. It's time for reflection and taking stock while the plants momentarily sleep. Life is pausing before becoming active again beneath the surface of the earth as a prelude to beginning the cycle once again.

We trust these rhythms of nature and appreciate that they show us how life is in its differing phases. "All shall be well, and all shall be well, and all manner of things shall be well," wrote the fourteenth-century Christian mystic Julian of Norwich in her *Revelations of Divine Love*. Julian differed from the authorities in the Medieval Church by preaching that "sin" should be seen as part of the learning process of life, not as an evil that needed forgiveness. She believed that to learn we must fail, and to fail we sin out of ignorance. According to her, God sees us as perfect and waits for the day when we become fully mature human beings. This is not unlike the Hindu idea that the Self, the Divine Spark, is at the core of every one of us. We have no need to acquire goodness because it is already within us. We simply have to remove the selfish ingrained habits that hide the Self.

I trust the seasons of my heart as I trust the rhythms of nature.

I am open to accepting that goodness is at the core of my being.

4. Learning the dance of life

Life is like a dance, and for the dance we need to be fluid, fearless, and aware. Everything in life is in a state of constant change, ebbing and flowing, waxing and waning, but we need to trust in the process of constant regeneration.

In Hinduism, Shiva, in the form of Nataraj, is the transforming god. In his cosmic dance, Shiva balances on one leg within a circle of flames, representing the continuous creation, maintenance, and destruction of the Universe. His right foot is poised over a demon representing ignorance, but Shiva's head is serene. As the archetypal dancer, Shiva represents the ever-changing life force with the myriads of worlds, galaxies, and beings taking shape and passing away. As the archetypal sage, he represents the absolute where all distinctions dissolve. This endless round of existence means beginnings and endings, with life renewing itself constantly.

Things may fall apart, but out of chaos something new is always being born. We cannot hold on to anything in life forever—we have to let go. Relationships dissolve, we lose parents, friends, and colleagues, possessions and homes can be destroyed, youth and beauty fade, fame and success are eclipsed, and our bodies wither and cease functioning. If we can learn to view life as a dance, however, and trust the life force within us to show us the way, wisdom and serenity can triumph over ignorance.

The martial arts like tai chi, aikido, judo, karate, and kendo help in physical, mental, emotional, and spiritual wellbeing, where the purpose of training is to enable the practitioner to respond in an appropriate manner when under attack. Thomas Crum uses the graceful martial art of aikido, often translated as "the way of harmonious spirit," or "the way of unifying life energy," in his well-known conflict resolution and stress management workshops. He advises us on not being afraid of the ups and downs of life: "Instead of seeing the rug pulled from under us, we can learn to dance on the shifting carpet."

I let go of what is no longer useful, knowing that
something new is being born.

I am learning to dance on a shifting carpet.

5. Heeding the messages

Our early ancestors, in common with indigenous peoples today who are closely attuned to nature, used their intuition far more than we do because they relied on it for survival. We tend to value rational, deductive, logical thinking far higher than intuition.

Messages come to us all the time in the form of coincidences, gut feelings, and dreams. The problem is that we're not always open to receiving them, or we miss them altogether, or fail to trust them even if we do hear them.

Some years ago I had an experience of synchronicity that gave me a powerful message. I had lost one of a pair of gold earrings that had been a present from my ex-husband. I was attached to these earrings (and still attached at some level to the memory of my relationship), so I decided to phone the jeweler to see whether the designer could make me one to match the remaining earring, which she agreed to do. After a few weeks, the jeweler rang me to say that she had taken delivery of the new earring and would be posting the pair to me. A few days later she phoned again, terribly apologetic. She'd had the earrings packed and ready to go, sitting on the counter, and the package had been stolen. Fortunately (or perhaps as it turned out, unfortunately), her insurance covered the earrings and she said she had already asked the designer to make another pair. I thought this was a strange thing to happen, but went along with it, and finally received the completely new earrings, which I did feel was symbolic because they were both totally new, even if the same design. However, within a short time I lost one of them again. This time I heard the message loud and clear. Enough was enough, and I went out and bought a completely different pair of earrings that I have to this day.

I came to realize that I had still been hanging on to the memory of my marriage, and that I had to work on dissolving the attachment totally. Something did indeed shift, and I was able to move on in my life, not just with new earrings, but ultimately to a new and happier relationship.

I'm open to receiving messages from the Universe.

I trust the messages I receive.

6. Letting the path be our teacher

No life unfolds without challenges, and from time to time we face a crisis that is so overwhelming that the pain is almost too much to bear. We tend to forget that we learn most from the experiences that cause us the greatest suffering. As the writer Ernest Hemingway wrote in his novel, *A Farewell to Arms*, about the suffering of the First World War, "The world breaks everyone and afterward many are strong at the broken places."

It is the broken pieces of ourselves that teach us what it is we need to learn and to grow. The problem is that when we are overwhelmed, like Dante's hero in *The Inferno*, we are lost and cannot see the way ahead. We know there is no going back and that we cannot alter what has happened. We can, however, decide how we will deal with the challenge. There is always an opportunity at the heart of suffering.

We have to learn to trust the path, with its twists and turns, however difficult it seems. We may only be able to move forward little by little, but the important thing is to keep making the effort. We have to trust that we can find a way through the darkness.

And the truth is, we usually do. When we trust life's process we begin to understand and accept that things are as they are. We learn to embrace life and see whatever is confronting us as both a lesson and a blessing, and in the unfolding we find courage and strength far greater than we thought we had. Our confidence grows as we make different choices, begin to have greater empathy with those around us, and start to feel more compassion. The path itself has been our teacher, and when, further along, we turn around and momentarily look back, we appreciate how far we've come and how much we have come to understand.

I choose to see life's challenges as both blessings and lessons.

I trust the path I'm on.

I embrace the opportunity to learn and grow.

Trusting life's process

7. Surrendering attachment

We often have something or someone in our lives that we need to let go of because we're being held back from living the life we really want for ourselves. We also need to surrender our attachment to our hopes for the future, trusting that once we're clear about what it is we want, and have articulated this, the outcome will be what we truly need for our growth.

I once did an effective shamanic practice that was helpful in enabling me to move on in my life. Shamanism flourished in ancient cultures, and many of the beliefs and practices had widespread similarities, and even today in indigenous cultures that is still the case. A shaman is an intermediary between ordinary reality and an altered state of consciousness, and journeys undertaken under the guidance of a shaman can be immensely liberating.

I was sitting in a tepee with my medicine friend at the base of Mount Shasta. Several Native American tribes had once lived within view of Mount Shasta, which dominates the Northern California landscape, rising to 3,000 meters. We had a small fire in the center of the tepee to keep us warm and to cook our supper.

We began with some drumming, followed by invocations to the spirits, and then meditation. My shaman guide then took me on a journey to the Lower World, handing me two darts, two sheets of paper, and a pen before I set off. My point of entry was a magical-looking tree I know, which is over 250 years old, with an almost completely hollow trunk. I descended through the trunk into a tunnel beneath the earth and made my way along until I came to a wide open space of meadows filled with wild flowers. I had been asked to write down on one sheet of paper three things that I wished to leave behind in my present life, and on the second sheet to write down three things I really wanted for the future. Once I had crystallized my thoughts, I was to take the first sheet with the things I wished to leave behind and attach it to one of the darts and bury it in the ground. The second sheet of paper with the things I wanted to happen in the future I was to attach to the second dart and then release it into the air. Having accomplished this, after a period of deep relaxation, I retraced my steps in the same manner and returned through the tunnel and my magic tree to the warmth of the tepee, giving thanks to the spirits.

The power of our imaginations can take us beyond our ordinary thinking and help us feel like we've passed through an initiation into a new life.

Trusting life's process

We've let go of what we need to let go of, whilst at the same time we've accepted that having asked for our wishes for the future, we need to release any expectation of anything other than what is good for our development.

I choose to leave behind those things I no longer need.
I focus on what I want for the future.

8. Receiving grace

Every so often we get a glimpse of the truth that everything is okay in our lives and that we're fine just as we are, because goodness is already at the heart of our being. We also get a sense that there is a purpose to our life, and that whatever happens is something we can learn from.

The great Bengali spiritual master, Ramakrishna Paramahamsa wrote: "The winds of grace are blowing all the time. You have only to raise your sail." If we are able to trust life's process, and the unfolding of our growth and understanding, through the varied experiences (good and bad) that we have, then we are open to the greater insight that grace bestows.

We can sense the life force at work all around us. Within our bodies our organs perform all kinds of amazing miracles on a daily basis, without us doing anything at all. Similarly, the sun, moon, and stars move in their orbits, we receive light, warmth, and rain, and the earth, forests, rivers, and seas are rich with abundant life. We accept that bountiful Nature provides for us.

Grace operates in our lives in the same way. When we surrender control, and gratefully open our hearts to the wonders of our lives, grace is constantly available to us.

However, to keep grace flowing, we have to play our part, and expressing and sharing gratitude is a big part of grace falling upon us like rain. We cannot receive without giving back and sharing. I'm fond of this little ritual, which is good to do at the end of a yoga or meditation session when we're practicing with others.

We hold hands and form two circles facing each other. The outer circle does not move, but the inner one does. Standing in the inner circle, each person, with arms outstretched and palms held upward, faces each person in the outer circle, with arms outstretched but palms facing down. Together we all sing the first line of the verse below, changing our hand position the opposite way round for the second line, then spreading our arms wide for the third line, and finally bowing and making the namaste greeting for the fourth line:

> From you I receive
> To you I give
> Together we share
> This is how we live.

We then pass on to the next person and repeat until everyone in the circles has greeted everyone else.

I am grateful for the moments of grace in my life.
I practice both receiving and giving.

9. Reassessing and rebuilding our lives

When a crisis erupts in our lives, we need to ask ourselves what is really going on. Whatever form it takes, it's usually some kind of wake-up call. However difficult the circumstances are, we need to trust that something isn't working and is trying to change—ultimately for our benefit. It may not seem so at the time, and often it might be a succession of crises that we're plunged into before we realize that life is forcing us to change. As we begin to accept this, we see that a different way of living is possible, and gradually we rebuild our lives with a new understanding.

They say troubles don't come singly, and I certainly found that to be the case at a time in my life when I was unhappy. First of all, I contracted cerebral malaria in East Africa and ended up being hospitalized for ten days. Secondly, my beautiful home was struck by lightning, causing damage to the central twelve-foot-high chimneys. Finally, I found myself trapped in New York on 9/11, close to the World Trade Center. Of course, I recognize that I was fortunate to escape any injury on that tragic and shocking occasion, but none the less it left me somewhat traumatized, unable to sleep for several nights, and I broke out in eczema over my entire body. These cumulative crises forced me to reassess my life, with the result that some weeks after my return to the UK I handed in my notice and changed the way I lived totally. The following year I found myself far happier and more fulfilled than I had been in a long time.

My friend Yvette is an example of someone who was forced to examine her successful but stressful life as a marketing executive in publishing. Diagnosed and treated for breast cancer, not once but twice, Yvette came to appreciate the healing power of dance during her recovery. Having trained in Egyptian belly dance, she decided to give up her career and follow her passion, and she is now very successful in teaching and performing traditional Egyptian and theatrical belly dancing. Her one-woman show, *Sequins on My Balcony*, offering a fresh perspective on breast cancer, body image, belly dance, and sisterhood, is gathering critical acclaim. Both funny and moving, her show celebrates the gorgeousness of women. Yvette is truly inspirational in this role she has created for herself and shares with us (also in her book of the same title), and is happier than she's ever been.

I trust life's process.

I am willing to accept that my life needs to change.

Chapter VIII

Living in the present moment

*You must have been warned against letting the hours
slip by; but some of them are golden only because we
let them slip by.*

J. M. BARRIE

Time is what we all seem to want more of. We regard
it as a precious commodity, and yet we don't seem
to know how to spend it wisely. On the one hand
we fill our lives to overflowing, trying to make the
most of time, but end up feeling time starved; on
the other hand, we deprive ourselves of time to do
nothing and seek distraction because we're not good
at being still and silent, with the result that we are
never able to recharge our batteries so that we can
feel time expanding.

Many of us are always rushing, cramming as much activity into the day as possible, multi-tasking, and absorbing huge quantities of information from every direction. Although modern technology and conveniences help us do everything more quickly, we still feel short on time. We expect to accomplish more now, much of which would have been inconceivable in previous generations. Even when we're supposed to be relaxing, we still crave stimulation rather than sitting quietly, so we watch TV, check our phones, or read a magazine. Is it any wonder we're no longer in touch with our feelings and are less connected to our fellow human beings than women used to be?

In the past people lived more in tune with the rhythms of nature. Without electricity there was a marked difference between night and day, and our experience of the seasons was sharper without central heating or air conditioning. Now we live by clock time—a construct that we've all signed up to, so that life can be organized and things can run smoothly, or so we think. But as the American novelist and poet William Faulkner reminded us, "Clocks slay time."

We need a different perspective on time, where we have a sense of timelessness. To gain that, we need to slow down and allow more stillness and quiet into our lives. Only then can we observe how distracted our minds are. If we choose to focus on our breathing, acknowledging our thoughts but letting them go as we stay focused, we begin to experience a sense of calm. We are able to bring more conscious awareness into our lives.

We begin to find that we can let go of time rather than needing more of it. Creating space frees us and helps us appreciate the beauty of simplicity, of ritual, and the peace of mind that mindfulness and meditation bring. We become aware of what we're really feeling, not labeling or judging, just accepting what arises. We don't spend our time regretting what happened yesterday or worrying about what might happen tomorrow. We're more able to live in the present moment, which enable us to experience joy.

As Thich Nhat Hanh, the Vietnamese Buddhist teacher, puts it, "The present moment is filled with joy and happiness. If you are attentive, you will see it."

1. Changing our perception of time

We all have our own experience of time. Time might fly if we're enjoying ourselves, it drags if we're ill or lonely, and if we're bored we might want to kill it. Time is elastic, but we try to control it and organize it with calendars, diaries, agendas, and deadlines.

We tend to think of time as linear because of our concept of progress. Compared to ancient cultures, we have a narrow view of time. For them, a circular idea of time prevailed. For the ancient pre-Columbian civilizations, the Native Americans, the Vedic civilization of India, and the Aborigine culture of Australia cyclical time was what mattered, and continues to matter where the ancient traditions are still practiced. There are also the great cycles of the astrological ages, bound up with mythology, psychology, and religion—an endless round of existence, with life renewing itself and evolving constantly.

When we see time in this way, with a more cosmic perspective of time, we free ourselves from the constraints of our modern notion of clock time. We can agree with the scientist Albert Einstein that "time is an illusion," and with the Beatle George Harrison that "all there ever is, is the now." Inner peace exists outside of time—there's no past and no future. We can rest in the present moment and connect with the wellspring at the center of our being, which is also at the heart of everything else that exists. The disparate parts of ourselves become harmonized, and we experience true joy.

Lao Tzu, the Chinese philosopher and author of the classic text *Tao Te Ching*, advises, "Practice not-doing and everything will fall into place."

We can choose to practice meditation or mindfulness and find the balance between being active and being still. When we take the time to look within and observe what's going on, we begin to appreciate the gift of each day. We can train ourselves to be aware and centered in our practice, and then life becomes a succession of moments in which we are constantly present.

I slow down and allow stillness into my life.
I take the time to look within.
I rest in the present moment.

2. Looking in the right place

We usually spend our time looking outside ourselves for what we hope will make us happy. Of course, it can be enjoyable to have wealth, relationships, possessions, and status—there's nothing wrong with that. When we chase after those things, however, making them our goal in the belief that we will be happy once we've attained them, we are going to be disappointed. Happiness can in no way be guaranteed, and is likely only to be fleeting. There is a

Tibetan saying: "Seeking happiness outside ourselves is like waiting for sunshine in a cave facing north."

It is only when we look within ourselves that emotional, psychological, and spiritual transformation can take place and that over time we find real joy. The spiritual master, Swami Muktananda, whose ashram at Ganeshpuri in India I was able to spend some time at when he was still alive, told a story about how we tend to look everywhere to find the joy we long for except the one place where we can find it.

The gods were arguing about where to hide the secret of life so that men and women would never find it.

"Bury it under a mountain," one god suggested, "they'll never find it there."

"No," said the other gods, "they'll find a way to dig beneath the mountains and find it."

"What about deep in the ocean?" another god suggested.

"No," said the gods, "they'll find a way to dive down and retrieve it."

After some time, one of the gods said, "Why not put it inside their hearts. They would never think of looking there."

And so the gods hid the secret of life within us.

*I accept that external pleasures cannot deliver pure
and lasting joy.*

I will look within to find joy.

3. Bringing conscious awareness into our lives

We spend much of our time living in a fairly unconscious manner, and yet we think of it as "normal" living. Underlying our lives is a sense of unease, even discontent, which Samuel Beckett captured memorably in his absurdist play *Waiting for Godot*: "You're on earth . . . there's no cure for that." It's the human condition. The Buddha saw and understood this, and prescribed a cure for availing ourselves of it by training the mind and developing conscious awareness.

Until we're ready to take this on board, we tend to drown out the unease with activity, or we suppress our tensions and anxieties with a glass or two of wine, watching TV, shopping, sex, or any of the other addictive behaviors we can find. We only temporarily assuage our dissatisfaction, however, and not for long.

Most of the time, we believe we're our ego, the self-image we've constructed for ourselves. If, however, we want to feel the joy that is our birthright, then we need to connect with the deeper part of ourselves that conscious awareness helps us access. Meditation is a powerful tool in achieving this, and our breath is an excellent starting point. We breathe in, we breathe out—it's as simple as that. When we are quiet and still and train our attention, we can see that thoughts and desires are continually arising, and that we label and judge what we like and don't like. As our minds begin to steady and focus, we experience the gradual slowing down of thoughts and emotions, and, even if only momentarily, we get a glimpse of the now and a taste of joy.

Ideally the practice of meditation becomes a daily habit, spilling over into our lives and giving them a different quality. We can connect with the breath at any time—we just have to remember to do so when we feel stressed or rattled. The Brahma Kumaris, a spiritual organization that teaches meditation, practices a nice reminder of how to reconnect to your breath. They call them "traffic stops." Every hour, on the hour, whatever you're doing, you pause and connect with the breath for a few moments. Pausing in our normal activities and turning inward really does help anchor us in awareness. It doesn't have to be formalized to be beneficial—we can just take some time to smell the flowers, to listen to birdsong, look at cobwebs glistening on leaves after rain, or enjoy the starlit sky—all these simple activities reconnect us to the life energy that pulses through us.

I take the time to develop conscious awareness.

I remember to pause to connect with the breath.

4. Moving beyond compulsive thinking

Our thoughts are constant and compulsive, giving rise to more thoughts and accompanying emotions. Although there's nothing wrong with thinking *per se*, the greater part of our thinking is actually negative and therefore harmful. We go over what happened in the past, and we judge and compare, with the result that we end up feeling sad, guilty, or resentful. Alternatively, we worry about the future, wondering what's going to happen, or imagining some awful happening that may never come about, but that our mind makes as real as if it had actually happened, so that we become fearful and unhappy. When we're constantly thinking about the past or the future, there's no way we're experiencing the present moment, and so we miss our opportunity for joy.

If instead we learn to direct our awareness to what's actually happening now, we can watch the thoughts and emotions come and go. We don't get entangled. We can choose to focus on our breath, or an image that is meaningful to us, or repeat a mantra (a word or phrase that holds meaning for us), so that we can allow the present moment to be as it is and prevent the mind from running away with itself.

When I'm wrestling with an issue, or my nerves are jangled, I go and pull some weeds. I find that after a short time I become so engrossed in what I'm doing that I forget entirely what was going around in my head. I enjoy the fresh air and the scents and sounds whilst I'm focusing on removing the offending weeds. Yes, I will have to return to deal with whatever I was grappling with before, but I feel renewed and refreshed and more able to tackle it.

When we're in the present moment, we don't feel stressed, angry, or afraid. All our anxieties evaporate, with the result that we have more strength and composure.

I direct my awareness to what is happening now.

I allow the present moment to be as it is.

I am renewed and refreshed by living in the present moment.

5. Restraint and keeping things simple

Our lives have become so complicated with the huge array of choices we have available, whether it's the products on the shelves in the supermarket or how we spend our leisure time. There have been material improvements in our way of life in the Western world over the last fifty to sixty years, which have brought benefits, and yet at the cost of our ability to enjoy the simple things in life, and at enormous cost to the planet and those less fortunate than us.

Rather than satisfying our needs, our material affluence means that we're constantly trying to satisfy our wants, and the temptations are endless. The problem with that is that there is always a desire for something else—once one desire has been fulfilled, another springs up in its place.

The idea of restraint doesn't appeal to us, and yet holding back from continually wanting to acquire or experience something is invaluable. The truth is that simpler pleasures ultimately give greater satisfaction than material benefits, simpler pastimes don't cost the earth, and a simpler lifestyle is likely to keep us healthier. We don't need too much luxury or instant this or that, whatever the marketing people tell us. We can choose to consume less and make our lives simpler.

If we don't take so much for granted and live more consciously, we can appreciate what we already have, even more so when we remember how little so many others in the world have. And isn't it astonishing, how happy young children so often are in the more deprived parts of the world, with nothing to play with except perhaps an old rubber tire, whilst our own children and grandchildren drown in a plethora of toys and games?

Instead of rushing out and buying something new when we think we want it, we can be more restrained—we can repair, repaint, or decorate. We can use our creative skills to sew a dress, knit a sweater, or bake a cake. We can become part of the sharing and caring culture growing up as a reaction to consumerism. Less consumption and greater consideration for others on the earth and for future generations will enable us to enjoy greater freedom and peace of mind. We don't have to chase after something that we feel is missing in our lives—we know that we have everything we need when we fully experience and appreciate the minutiae of each day.

I choose to consume less and make my life simpler.

I appreciate what I already have.

I know that I have everything I need.

6. Practicing silence and solitude

Whilst for Shakespeare silence was "the perfectest herald of joy," the poet and writer May Sarton described it as "a fabulous gift." Silence and solitude are vital for reflection and for enabling us to get in touch with the wellspring of joy within us.

All too often our lives are subjected to a barrage of external noise—phones, traffic, radios, machinery, airplanes, and sirens. But there is also the noise that goes on relentlessly in our heads—our minds are mostly busy from morning to night with their ceaseless chatter.

We do have opportunities for periods of silence throughout the day as we go about our ordinary lives—in the shower, in our cars, whilst cooking, or before falling asleep—we can choose to do these things in silence rather than talk or listen to the radio or music. Extending our periods of silence and solitude and practicing inner silence can become a habit, so that we are able to find deep peace within us, where there is no time, only the present moment. As the inspirational self-study course *A Course in Miracles* reminds us:

> There is a silence
> into which the world cannot intrude.
> There is an ancient peace
> you carry in your heart
> and have not lost.

Many in the past have sought peace and tranquility far removed from the distractions of the world. The ancient rishis of India withdrew to live in caves in the Himalayas, the Desert Fathers went out into the Egyptian wilderness, and the Irish monks set out to sea in their curraghs. It's not just hermits and mystics, however, who valued silence and solitude—so too have writers, composers, artists, philosophers, and scientists like Goethe, Mozart, and Einstein. There are also those who have thrived in enforced solitude. Boethius wrote *The Consolation of Philosophy* in the sixth century whilst incarcerated in Pavia, John Bunyan wrote much of *Pilgrim's Progress* in prison, whilst Gandhi and Nelson Mandela in the twentieth century also used their imprisonment beneficially.

When we are able to still our minds, and are in touch with our true selves, we are able to hear "the still small voice" of guidance. Only where there is no time, no past, no future, only the present moment, are we connected to the Source of life that connects us all, and can find the answers to all our questions.

I choose to rest in the deep peace within.
I listen to the still small voice of guidance.
I am connected to the Source of life.

7. Developing our capacity for patience

"Hurry sickness" is a modern disease—we live frenetically, travel far greater distances than ever before, and are bombarded with information far more than in previous centuries. So when we're forced to stop and wait in traffic jams or check-out lines, or when there's a flight delay or slow service in a restaurant, we become impatient. When we're sick, we want the doctor to give us something so we can get back to "normal" life as quickly as possible. We can't wait for a bad mood to lift, the weekend to come, or a new relationship to enter our lives. We're not good at enduring uncomfortable situations, we grumble about inefficiency and incompetence, and we are not at ease with ourselves for any length of time.

Even if we're used to practicing yoga or meditation, we can get up from our session only to lose the calm we've acquired as soon as something or someone presses our buttons. We react without thinking, instead of patiently working out what our response should be.

We need to develop our capacity for patience, which begins with training ourselves to slow down and pay attention. It also requires us to accept things as they are, without wishing them to meet our expectations. And similarly with our relationship with others, we need to be aware of and accepting of difference.

We can become more resilient and enjoy the benefits of practicing. We're no longer agitated if someone is late, we become more relaxed, and we stop trying to control situations. We become more accepting of our partner's foibles, and appreciate his or her strengths more, so that we end up having more loving exchanges. And patience at work pays dividends, in better relations with our colleagues, more successful negotiations, and less feeling under pressure.

We have many opportunities during the course of a day to practice patience, and when we do, we can take deep breaths, we can say our mantra, we can appreciate everything that we're involved in, and we can send out love and blessings to others. The more aware we become, the more we will be able to deal skillfully with situations that would have made us anxious and frustrated in the past.

I choose to slow down and pay attention.

I am willing to accept things as they are.

I practice patience and handle situations skillfully.

8. Creating ritual and sanctuary

Religious traditions have always been strong on ritual and sanctuary, with sacraments, rites of passage, ceremonies, seasonal celebrations, and sacred dance and music, but our twenty-first century world has far less meaningful ritual than in the past. We now have fewer reminders of the sacred in everyday life where once they were commonplace.

All ritual is symbolic, helping to prepare our minds and bodies for a shift in awareness. The original meaning of the Greek-derived word for symbol was "bringing together." Ritual helps us focus on what is truly important; it helps orient us and connects us with the Source of life.

We can, of course, create our own rituals if we don't necessarily want to participate in those of the Church or other institutions, but we need to ensure that they are meaningful if they are to help us live joy-filled lives. Daily rituals hold things together so that we feel deeply connected with life. Instead of beginning each day in a headlong rush, a slow start sets the tone for the day. Getting up a little earlier before others are awake, so that we have a little quiet time, is beneficial, regardless of the fact that we have a busy program for the day. Regular meditation, yoga, tai chi, or prayer and reflection help us maintain a sense of connection with the flow of life.

We can create our own sanctuary at home. It doesn't have to be a whole room, a corner of a room will suffice, but somewhere we can remind ourselves of our true nature. Whether we have an altar, a statue, a photograph of a spiritual teacher, flowers, a pebble, incense, or a candle is entirely a matter of personal choice. Even in the office we can have something to remind us to be mindful. We might also choose places special to us outside, such as a garden, a forest, or a beach where we can retreat to, walk, and reflect. We can also enjoy the rituals of sharing a meal together with family or friends, and especially for birthdays and anniversaries and seasonal feasts and festivals.

I love the seasonal celebrations, and the rituals of church and temple, but I also enjoy my own personal rituals of lighting a candle and incense before I settle down to meditate. More secular rituals, such as my morning cup of coffee, when I pause and reflect and count my blessings, or when I come in from gardening and clean up and put my tools away, thankful for the fresh air and exercise and the opportunity to be working with nature, help ground and connect me.

I create my personal reminders of my connection to the Source of life.

I find joy through the rituals in my life.

9. Living each day as if it's the only one we have

We often act as if life is a dress rehearsal and spend more time than makes sense trying to get somewhere where life can really begin. It may be putting up with a boss we don't like, hoping to land the perfect job in the future; or being unhappy in a close relationship that we know isn't good for us, and wishing that we could meet someone else; or simply being so fed up with our lives that all we're doing is looking forward to our holiday. The danger is that we can spend the greater proportion of our lives anticipating a time when things will be as we want them to be, meanwhile missing all the precious moments that are there before us. We long for the future to come and miss the treasure that is today.

"Saving for best" is another manifestation of not living in the present moment, and also of not valuing ourselves enough. We buy a new dress and it hangs in the wardrobe waiting for the right occasion. It's true, there's nothing nicer than having something crisply new to put on for that special occasion, and yes, it's not always practical to dress up every day if we're cooking, gardening, or dealing with small children and sticky fingers. But how do we actually feel if we live in our scruffy old jeans and t-shirts all the time, with our hair scrunched up in a ponytail? There's nothing more special than today, so why not find time to make ourselves feel good by making the most of ourselves, even if only for part of the day?

I remember a friend clearing out her mother's home after she had died to find drawers of beautiful silk underwear still in its tissue wrapping paper and clearly never worn. What was she waiting for? How many of us are daft enough to save something for best, only to find it looks dated or no longer fits when we finally put it on? I'm afraid I have to admit to being guilty on this one occasionally.

Our ambitions can also be symptomatic of a tendency to live for tomorrow. Whilst we're striving to reach some goal we've set ourselves, we may be less aware of the weeks, months, and years that are zooming by, and the moments of joy we miss because we're overly focused at the expense of other things on where we want to get to. Of course it's not wrong to have ambitions, but not at the expense of living now. We don't know what lies ahead, so there's no point in not living each day as if it's the only one we have, because it might just be that.

Living in the present moment

I focus on the treasure that is today.
I choose to make each day special.

10. Accepting things as they are

Although we often have to face up to the necessity for change in our lives, there is much we cannot change. We can change our thoughts, our habits, and our behaviors, but we cannot change what has happened in the past, the cards life has dealt us, or the choices we've made.

Practicing stillness and quiet and endeavoring to live in the present moment help us with acceptance, whereas looking outside doesn't. As Kabir, the sixteenth century mystic poet and saint of India, puts it:

Don't go outside your house to see the
   flowers.
My friend, don't bother with that excursion.
Inside your body there are flowers.
One flower has a thousand petals.
That will do for a place to sit.
Sitting there you will have a glimpse of
   beauty

inside the body and out of it,
before gardens and after gardens.

In that "glimpse of beauty" lies eternity, and this is
what we long for. We know that our lives are short,
and since we have no way of knowing when our time
will be up, we need to live with the acceptance of
things being the way they are. The Koran tells us,
"Paradise is nearer to you than the thongs of your
sandals." We can live our lives fully by appreciating
the moments that make up each day, living in the
flow of joy and letting the light of understanding fill
our hearts. Rabindranath Tagore, the Bengali poet,
novelist, composer, artist, and so much more, has
been an inspiration to me for many years of my own
journey:

> Your light, my light, world-filling light, the
> dancing center of my life, the sky breaks forth,
> the wind runs wild, and laughter passes over the
> earth.
> The butterflies have spread their sails to
> glide upon the seas of light; the lilies and the
> jasmine flowers surge on the crest of the waves
> of light.
> Now heaven's river drowns its banks, and
> floods of joy have run abroad; now mirth has

spread from leaf to leaf, and gladness without measure comes.

I accept that things are the way they are.
I appreciate the moments that make up each day.
I choose to live in the flow of life.

Chapter IX

Appreciating life's blessings

Gratitude unlocks the fullness of life. It turns what we have into enough, and more. It turns denial into acceptance, chaos to order, confusion to clarity. It can turn a meal into a feast, a house into a home, a stranger into a friend. Gratitude makes sense of our past, brings peace for today, and creates vision for tomorrow.

MELODY BEATTIE

Appreciation of all that we have in our lives plays an important role in our health and happiness. Research carried out at the Greater Good Science Center at the University of California by Robert A. Emmons and his colleagues has shown that there are definite physical, psychological, and social benefits to practicing gratitude. When we appreciate life's blessings, the result is stronger immune systems, fewer aches and pains, lower blood pressure, improved sleep, and less chance of heart attack. Psychological benefits include less depression, less stress, a greater experience of positive emotions, and a sense of wellbeing. There are also distinct social advantages to practicing gratitude, because when we acknowledge the good things in our lives and give thanks for them, we are connecting to something larger than ourselves as individuals, and are also more likely to feel empathy and compassion, be more forgiving, and more generous and outgoing.

Gratitude is that sense of thankfulness and wonder that we feel when we know how blessed we are, and it is an expression of love. Og Mandino, the inspirational author and speaker, offered wise words to set the tone for each day:

> I will greet this day with love in my heart. And how will I do this? Henceforth will I look on all things with love and I will be born again. I will love the sun for it warms my bones; yet I will love the rain for it cleanses the spirit. I will love the light for it shows me the way; yet I will love the darkness for it shows me the stars. I will welcome happiness for it enlarges my heart, yet

I will endure sadness for it opens my soul. I will acknowledge rewards for they are my due; yet I will welcome obstacles for they are my challenge.

It's worth welcoming and appreciating everything that comes into our lives, and making gratitude a habit. We can appreciate the past, the present, and the future. When we appreciate the past, we're grateful for our parents and childhood, and all the experiences we've had that have made us who we are. We can appreciate the present, enjoying any good fortune that comes to us, but if life is challenging, we can also appreciate the good things that we do have in life. We can also be grateful for what lies ahead, facing the future without fear, and knowing that much of it depends on our thoughts and behaviors today.

1. Giving thanks on a daily basis

From time to time we're blessed to feel ecstatically happy—a major promotion we've been wanting, a wonderful celebration with family and friends, or an exciting new relationship. It's not difficult to experience a sense of gratitude and give thanks on such occasions.

These are external circumstances that have made us happy, however, and rather than waiting for something to feel grateful for, we can make it a habit to practice feeling appreciative of what we already have, so that we feel happy even when there's no external reason. This will also stand us in good stead when times are difficult and we find it harder to remember to be thankful. If we have cultivated the practice of giving thanks on a daily basis, then we can counteract automatically any negativity with appreciation of the good things we enjoy. Research has demonstrated that it's possible to cultivate "an attitude of gratitude," and as with any other skill it can be learned and developed until it becomes second nature.

We have so many reasons to be thankful each day. For a start, we've enjoyed a night's rest, and another day of opportunity stretches before us, and we have no idea what it may bring. Thich Nhat Han, the Vietnamese teacher and writer, puts it beautifully: "Waking up this morning, I smile. Twenty-four brand new hours are before me. I vow to live fully in each moment and to look at all beings with eyes of compassion."

If we take a few moments before we get out of bed in the morning to think about all the good things in our lives, we will find there are always more than we imagine. If we find it hard to do this, then we can begin with just one thing and focus on it. If we feel really grateful for just this one thing, we find that something shifts, and we begin to find more reasons to give thanks, until they come thick and fast.

Another practice that is helpful is to keep a journal and write down every evening all the things that we're grateful for that have happened over the course of the day, however small. We can also give thanks for the miracle of our bodies and minds, for our homes, family and friends, for fresh water to drink, the food we eat, the wine we share, the clothes we wear, for everything that makes life comfortable . . . Once we are alert and aware, then we see how much there really is to be grateful for. Over time, if we do this conscientiously, we begin to see changes in our attitude. We find ourselves embracing life more and we're more accepting of ourselves and others.

I am grateful for _____.
I welcome this new day with all its opportunities.
I give thanks for the miracle of life.

Appreciating life's blessings

2. Seeing the bigger picture

When we're feeling sad, depressed, or lonely, the world appears grey to us, and we miss the wonders that surround us because our thoughts and problems weigh us down. There is no greater antidote to this, however, than reminding ourselves of the positives in our lives, even if we might find it difficult to begin with.

We need to shift our perspective from what we see as missing in our lives to focusing on what we do have. We take so much for granted and forget how fortunate we really are. Starting with the smallest of things when we wake up—the warmth of our beds, the coffee we're about to make, the phone call we're expecting from a friend; we can be grateful for who we are and the life we have; and we can extend this outward, to the beauty and abundance of the earth and this extraordinary unfolding Universe of which we are a part. Although the world has its tragedies and horrors, it's also a place of goodness, plenty, and opportunity. We can remind ourselves that we live in a world of unlimited potential.

When we see that we do have reasons to be thankful, we begin to feel differently. We see more clearly, noticing things we might have missed before. We become less preoccupied with ourselves and real-

ize the connection we have with others. We appreciate having them in our lives, seeing the best in them,
and being kinder as a result. We no longer want to
criticize or complain, we don't feel hard done by,
or get stressed about things that are not important.
We see the bigger picture, not the narrowed-down
world of scarcity and lack that our egos created, but
a world of abundance. Instead of regretting the past
and worrying about the future, we're more able to
live in the present moment, feeling grateful for the
fullness of life now.

I know how blessed I am to be here.

*I appreciate that the world is a place of goodness,
plenty, and opportunity.*

I open myself to abundance.

3. Having enough and realizing that nothing is lacking

Our consumer-driven culture thrives on us always
wanting more, and so it tries to persuade us that we
really will be happier, feel more secure, or be more

attractive if we buy a particular product, whether it's a smarter car, insurance, or the latest face cream.

Similarly, because we live in a competitive society and our identity matters to us, we're always striving to achieve more—more status, wealth, or opportunities for pleasure and adventure. Lack and a sense of scarcity are endemic in our materialistic society, and it's all too easy to focus on what we don't have, rather than on what we do. If we only paid attention to all that life offers us, we would know that we have enough. "Enough" is when our needs are met, and our needs are basically very simple—health, loving relationships, a home, a job, or something that gives us a sense of purpose and meaning. It's important to our wellbeing that our needs are met, but our wants are what cause us problems. Our wants are legion, and when one want is satisfied, we're happy for a while, but then we find ourselves desiring something else.

When we stop the constant wishing for something else and take stock of everything we already have, there is a feeling of abundance. Lao Tzu, the legendary Taoist philosopher of ancient China, advises us: "Be content with what you have; rejoice in the way things are. When you realize there is nothing lacking, the whole world belongs to you."

Gratitude turns on its head the idea that we don't have enough. When we appreciate what we do have on a regular basis, we realize how rich we are. We can experience happiness now, not at some point in the future when what we wish for might, or might not, be fulfilled, and we are more trusting that our needs will always be taken care of. We radiate joy when our sense of appreciation and abundance overflows.

I have enough and am thankful.
I can trust that my needs will always be met.
I appreciate life's abundance.

4. Being appreciative of ourselves and others

We all need to feel appreciated from time to time. Thanks, praise, and compliments make us feel valued and respected for our efforts, whether it's in our homes, our workplaces, or our communities. They contribute to our sense of wellbeing, help motivate us, and can also help give us courage and strength to deal with life's challenges.

Before we can genuinely appreciate others, we need to value ourselves. This means accepting ourselves as we are, grateful for all the experiences we've had that have made us who we are, and happy with what we've achieved so far. We also need to feel that we deserve life's blessings. When there is no sense of fear, guilt, or unworthiness, we are more able to appreciate others and feel at ease about showing that appreciation.

Relationships flourish with appreciation. When we genuinely appreciate someone because they've gone out of their way to do something thoughtful and kind for us, we feel warmth toward them and want to let them know how much it means that they have taken the trouble to make us happy. The recipient of our gratitude then feels appreciative because we've demonstrated that we value them and made them feel understood. It's very bonding to appreciate another, it nourishes intimacy, and we both benefit from a sense of self-worth.

If we make it a habit to tell our partners, friends and family, and colleagues how much we appreciate their help and caring, or how much they mean to us and what a difference it makes, then appreciation grows. When problems arise in a relationship, instead of blaming, criticizing, or getting mad, we can handle the situation more positively with appreciation of their good points. We need to work at getting kindness and appreciation flowing back and forth. Smiling is always good, and a sense of humor is even better. A research study at Loma Linda University has demonstrated that laughter produces an abundance of gamma brain waves similar to those found in people who meditate. Shared laughter makes us all feel good and helps put things into perspective.

I can smile at everyone I meet today.
I choose to be kind and appreciative of others.
I choose to have more laughter in my life.

5. Asking and receiving

There is something very simple that we need to remember to do, and that is to ask for help and guidance, and to be open to receiving blessings. When we're confused and troubled we tend to forget this, yet the Source of strength and comfort is always available to us. We attract what we ask for and what we consistently focus our attention on. As Mary Webb, the English novelist and poet, wrote: "The well of Providence is deep. It is the buckets we bring that are small."

If we can sit quietly, turning our attention inward, and endeavor to still the turmoil of thoughts and emotions, all we need do is ask and trust. It can be a heartfelt request to the Universe or a prayer that means something to us, but we can be sure that guidance will be there for us if we are genuinely open to receiving it, preferably with a large bucket.

Messages can come to us in so many ways when we open our hearts and remain alert—it may be a book we come across, a phone call from out of the blue at the precise moment we need it, a story we hear that echoes some part of our own, or a business card given to us—something that speaks to us after we've asked for guidance.

Some of us believe we have guardian angels who give us messages of hope and inspiration as well as keeping an eye on us. Certainly there have been occasions in my life when I have felt the protecting arms of a guardian angel. I seem to have been blessed to escape from some dangerous situations in my time, and have had a strong sense that this was not chance or coincidence. Relief and overwhelming gratitude on these occasions have enabled me to feel a greater sense of "The Force" being with me, and to trust that it will be there in the future whatever the situation and the outcome may be.

As important as it is to remember to ask for help, it is also important to acknowledge and give thanks for the guidance and blessings received, rather than forgetting all about it once the danger has passed. When we wake in the morning, or before we go to sleep at night, we can give thanks for all the help we've been given, and the proof we've had of a benign influence in our lives, which is guiding us every step of the way.

I am willing to ask for help and guidance.

I am open to receiving blessings.

I am grateful for all the good things I receive.

6. Opening to wonder and miracles

There are so many things to marvel at in our world if our hearts can be open to them, and if we can see them without judging and distorting through our thoughts and opinions. It was Albert Einstein, father of the Theory of Relativity, who said, "There are only two ways to live your life. One is as though nothing is a miracle. The other is as though everything is a miracle."

Starting with ourselves we can appreciate the miracle of our body and its functioning, which we tend to take for granted until something goes wrong.

The heart, the brain, the organs for digestion and elimination, the senses, all the myriads of cells, nerves, muscles, and tissues, cooperate through an amazing system of interconnections to carry out the necessary functions they perform. And we are able to walk, dance, sing, play tennis, make love, and do 1,001 things as a result. Awesome, really!

This amazing orchestration is also mirrored in the world around us. Beyond ourselves, we are part of larger wholes—family, community, the whole of humanity and life on the planet. Our existence within the miraculous living organism of Gaia is certainly something to appreciate. We are all moved by the beauty and magnificence of the natural world with its mountains, plains, forests, rivers, and seas, teeming with life and energy.

Using our senses, we can wonder at the miracle of life evident all around us on a daily basis. I'm blessed with a garden, but just as rewarding, if we don't have one, is a walk in the park or the countryside, or along the beach, or in woodland. Even walking down a street in the heart of a city or town there is much to marvel at. We can look up at the sky, at the architecture of the buildings surrounding us; maybe there are a few cherry trees with their magnificent frothy blossoms, or some colorful flower displays hanging in doorways or on windowsills. We can look at people, endlessly fascinating as they go about their lives, each with their own story written on their faces. If we're confined indoors because of ill-health or old age, a plant can remind us of our connection to the miracle of life. Growing bulbs or seeds on a windowsill indoors always thrills me! And we can be thankful for the possessions and photographs we have around us that evoke memories and give us pleasure. We can listen to uplifting music. We can share the space with friends and family when they visit us. We can be thankful that we are alive.

Wherever we are, there are things to delight us. We only have to be aware and use our senses and open our hearts. When we are able to appreciate and give thanks for life as it is, and when we revel in the here and now, our hearts are filled with joy.

I appreciate the miracle of my body.

I am grateful for all the wonders of life that surround me.

I open my heart to the magnificence of the Universe.

Appreciating life's blessings

7. Rejoicing in the small things and celebrating the big

Most mornings after I've completed my yoga and meditation practice, I feel so grateful for the silence that surrounds me. I enjoy lingering over my breakfast coffee, piping hot and strong, with just the right amount of whole milk, and in a particularly attractive cup and saucer that I've had for many years. These rituals with which I begin my day are important to me, and I'm grateful that I'm in a position to enjoy them.

As the day unfolds, I take time to look at the sky and watch the clouds. I will certainly wander around my garden and admire whatever is in bloom, whilst also making a mental note of what needs to be done. Juxtapositions of shape, color, and texture delight me, and I admire the small miracle of a spider's web glistening after rain, or I enjoy the dancing of butterflies over my lavender border. I can watch an array of birds, from the enormous heron that comes to steal the fish from my pond, to the tiniest wrens darting into their nest in the bush beneath my kitchen windowsill. Squirrels chase each other across the lawn and up into the fir trees, and the occasional hedgehog is a welcome visitor, though much as I love the rabbits I tell them they're only allowed to eat the grass! I love it when I'm digging and a robin comes to sit near me and sing, even though I know he's only waiting for the worms, or when I'm surprised by a rustle and one of the many frogs leaps out of the undergrowth. I love to hear the sound of the water as it runs through the stream, and over the rocks, and to watch the dragonflies hovering over the pond.

Through the seasons I marvel at each display of color and the varied scents from trees, shrubs, and flowers. When the snowdrops in my tiny woodland garden begin to emerge in winter, I'm ecstatic and praise them for their resilience and beauty. Then there is the ethereal pink and white blossom of the orchard in springtime, the magic of midsummer roses and lilies perfuming the evening air, and the harvest of fruit and vegetables that my efforts, in collaboration with nature, provide. For me these simple pleasures are all gifts to be thankful for, and part of the patchwork of my days.

As well as the gentle rhythms of the seasons, I enjoy the big seasonal festivals and celebrations; times for sharing with family and friends, heartwarming experiences with plenty to eat and drink, and therapeutic conversation and laughter.

As we age it's important to celebrate the milestones of major birthdays, anniversaries, reunions, and the weddings of the younger generations, as well as the birth of grandchildren. Such moments help us appreciate the journey we're still on. We can take a step back and review what we've accomplished that has made a difference and that we've found fulfilling, grateful that we've had the opportunities. We can celebrate and cherish and give thanks for all those who share our lives in some way, providing us with love and companionship, and contributing to our growth.

Celebrating both the big events and the dreams realized is matched by savoring the minutiae of our daily lives. Appreciating all the positives that have made our lives rich brings both joy and peace of mind.

🦋

I'm grateful for life's daily miracles.

I give thanks for life's milestones, which remind me of the opportunities I've enjoyed.

I give thanks for all those who share my life.

8. Increasing our generosity

As our appreciation of life and the blessings we enjoy grows, we're more trusting of the Source from which everything comes, and more cognizant of the flow of receiving and giving. Instead of blocking this flow because of a sense of lack or scarcity, we feel a sense of real inner wealth and a Universe of plenty. We become naturally more generous, since giving comes out of this feeling of abundance.

When we are genuinely generous, our hearts are open and we want to help one another, recognizing that we're all part of humanity. Connecting with others reminds us that we can make a difference. We can give of our time, our money, our possessions, but we can also give of our care, attention, and love. Whether we're giving some of our possessions or money to charitable causes, giving time to help a friend move house, or offering to help a stranger in distress, there are more than enough opportunities to give of ourselves without expecting anything in return. We can give a smile, a compliment, encouragement, affection, and we can practice random acts of kindness. I know one man who gives away tiny red roses he has made to everyone he meets.

All the religious traditions have emphasized the importance of the dynamics of giving with no expectation of reward. *The Bhagavad Gita*, one of the most popular Indian spirituality classics, describes authentic generosity as a gift: "When it is given from the heart to the right person at the right time and at the right place, and when we expect nothing in return."

Appreciating life's blessings

233

We need never feel in any sense diminished by giving, and if we can give something extra, something more perhaps than we can afford to give, even better. C. S. Lewis, the Christian writer and creator of *The Chronicles of Narnia*, when asked about giving, counseled: "I do not believe one can settle how much we ought to give. I am afraid the only safe rule is to give more than we can spare."

What is true is that the more we give, the more we're involved in the flow of the Universe's energy, and the more we ourselves will receive.

I can make a difference by being generous.

I can give without expecting anything in return.

I believe that the more I give, the more I receive.

9. Realizing how even loss can be a blessing

How often have we found in life that something we thought was a disaster at the time was actually a blessing in disguise: the end of a relationship, unemployment, an illness, or even a tragic accident? Somehow it turned out that something good came out of the situation and we had an opportunity to rise to the challenge and turn a negative into a positive. Elizabeth Kübler-Ross, the Swiss psychiatrist who wrote the groundbreaking book *On Death and Dying*, wrote: "Know that everything in this life has a purpose. There are no mistakes, no coincidences, all events are blessings given to us to learn from."

There are countless examples of people who have experienced terrible losses or been traumatized by tragedies who have gone on to find reasons for living and to help others.

Heather Abbot was caught up in the Boston marathon terrorist bombings and lost her leg. A blade now allows her to pursue her passion for running. But for Heather it took this experience to enable her to see how important it is to focus on what you have rather than what you don't have. Heather admits it was devastating to lose her leg, but appreciates that she still has her life. She feels she owes it to herself to move on with her life in a positive way.

Two young brothers, Rob and Paul Forkan, have done just that. They lost their parents in the Asian tsunami of 2004 while they were staying at a resort in Sri Lanka, but managed to survive by clinging to a tree. In 2011 they founded Gandys, a flip-flop company where 10 percent of the profits go to help orphans in developing countries.

Perhaps most inspiring of all is the story of Joost van der Westhuizen, the Springbok's leading rugby player, who now has motor neurone disease. The South African now fights a campaign to raise awareness and build the first specialist unit in South Africa for sufferers of MND. He recognized that he had a choice of staying at home and dying, or living a purpose-driven life, and has defied the odds by staying positive in spite of being, in effect, a prisoner in his body.

Thich Nhat Hanh, the Vietnamese Zen Buddhist priest who lived through the war in Vietnam and helped the victims of that war, is very well acquainted with suffering, but counsels:

> Life is filled with suffering, but it is also filled with many wonders, like the blue sky, the sunshine, the eyes of a baby. To suffer is not enough. We must also be in touch with the wonders of life . . . Wherever we are, any time, we have the capacity to enjoy the sunshine, the presence of each other, even the sensation of our breathing. We can be in touch with these things right now. It would be a pity if we are only aware of suffering.

Appreciating the good in our lives is not so very difficult, but if there has been a major catastrophe in our lives, it's far more challenging to reframe the situation into something positive. It takes immense guts. It's why we need to make gratitude a habit so that it becomes as natural in our lives as breathing. Then, when setbacks or tragedies occur, we can find the strength to continue living, and we are motivated to do something to relieve the suffering of others.

I am glad to be alive.

I know that life is always worth living.

Chapter X

Finding our
unique purpose

*Each of us will hear a different voice, one that is
unique to us, and we will each be called in a different
direction. But once heard, we must find the courage
to reunite with that voice and trust where it leads. It
is the voice of our truest nature. If we fail to hear its
inner call, we will be less than we might have been,
and we will never truly find peace and a sense of
completeness.*

MARILYN BARRETT

Whoever we are, and whatever our life may be like,
we all wonder at some point whether there's more
to it than we're currently experiencing. We have a
nagging sense that we have potential that hasn't yet

been realized, that we're capable of more, and that life could be richer.

We each have a unique combination of talent, skills, and experience that we long to use in expressing ourselves in some meaningful way and sharing with others. Our life's purpose, which we came into this world with, unfolds within us, whether we're aware of it or not, and at some point it calls us to be what we were born to be. As Paul Tillich, one of the most influential Christian theologians of the twentieth century, put it: "Man is asked to make of himself what he is supposed to become to fulfill his destiny."

Joseph Campbell famously urged us to "follow our bliss." Campbell was the groundbreaking explorer of mythology, well known for his idea of the hero's (or heroine's!) journey that features in all myths, regardless of culture, time, or place, and also is the plot of many epic novels or films, from *The Lord of the Rings* to *The Wizard of Oz*. By "bliss" Campbell meant the state of flow that we experience when we are doing something that we love and it feels so right that it seems almost effortless, and time stands still and we forget any worries that we might have had. When we're in this state, doors seem to open for us and help seems to come from every direction. It feels like it's meant to be and we feel alive and energized.

We sense that connection to something larger than ourselves, the Source of all life.

The call is the start of the heroine's journey, but if we're too fearful to take a step into the unknown and choose not to heed this call, preferring instead to cling to the security and comfort we erroneously think we have, our lives remain unfulfilled and lack joy. In the Gnostic Gospel of Thomas, found at Nag Hammadi, one of the sayings attributed to Jesus is, "If you bring forth what is within you, what you bring forth will save you. If you do not bring forth what is within you, what you do not bring forth will destroy you."

We have to let our unique purpose unfold. We need to heed the call and be courageous enough to follow the path where it takes us. We can choose to live our lives differently, trusting that there will be help and guidance for us, so that we can fulfil our destiny. Ultimately we find that it is in dedicating our skills and talents in service to others that we will experience true joy. Albert Schweitzer, who dedicated his life to helping others, most famously at his hospital at Lambaréné in Gabon, advised, "The only ones among you who will be really happy are those who have sought and found how to serve."

Finding our unique purpose

1. Asking the right questions

We live so much of our lives on autopilot, caught up in surviving, yet feeling that there's something missing. We sense somehow that our lives need to change—first we may hear soft whispers, then louder rumblings, and then suddenly there comes a point at which we get a thunderous wakeup call, most likely in the form of a crisis that could be to do with our health, or a relationship breakdown, or an inability to meet our debts. Forced to take stock, we look in the mirror and ask ourselves *Who am I? What's my life about? Where am I headed?*

We realize that we're out of touch with who we really are. We've been running so hard, we haven't given the time to explore what it is we really want out of life. The only way we can find answers to our questions and find our authentic selves is to turn within. Having identified with our ego, the image of who we think we are and the role we play, rather than being in touch with the core of our being, we're disconnected from the Source of life. We may well have had goals and objectives, but did they truly reflect our passions? They may well have been others' goals impressed upon us, and of course, once we've achieved them, we're no longer sure this is what we want, because they are not reflecting who we really are.

We need to take time to get to know ourselves better, and whether it's through meditation and mindfulness, or through psychotherapy or counseling, when we do give ourselves the time and space to explore the feelings that arise, the quality of our lives begins to change.

Finding our true purpose in life involves getting to know our personality traits, our values, our skills, and our talents. As we reflect on what it is we most love to do, we can begin to explore how we can express our passion and how we can make it the focus of our lives, reclaiming our authentic power. Maya Angelou, author, poet, and civil rights activist, was very clear about her purpose: "My mission isn't merely to survive, but to thrive; and to do so with some passion, some compassion, and some style."

We may feel we want to participate in some movement for change in society, or it may be that we want to create something of benefit to our culture, or to leave something of value behind. We may decide that we want to work for a charitable organization, care for the sick in a hospital, or teach young children in a school. We might want to be a writer, a musician, or an artist. We may be perfectly happy being a mother bringing up children. It doesn't matter what it is, the most important thing is to find something we totally enjoy and to which we can devote our time and energy.

Whatever we choose, we have an opportunity to deal with people in a meaningful way once we know that this is what we're truly happy doing. We can make someone feel better by treating them well, being interested in them, and giving good service. We can make a difference, as the poet and novelist D. H. Lawrence illustrated when he wrote about "kindling the life force where it was not, even if it's only in the whiteness of a washed pocket handkerchief."

I am willing to explore what it is I want out of life.
I am living my passion.
I can make a difference.

2. Trusting our unique purpose is unfolding

Instinctively, we feel that our lives must have meaning, and that there is some guiding principle to live by, rather like having our own north star to guide us. We have to follow where our passion takes us and not let fear and self-limiting beliefs paralyze us, or allow opposition from others to divert us from embarking on our journey.

Artist Lily Yeh felt compelled to find more meaning in her life, even though she had taught painting and art history for thirty years, raised a family, and felt generally blessed with her life. She felt "the call," and her path led her to the broken neighborhood of North Philadelphia, where together with an unemployed man and an ex-drug dealer she created an art park. This became the Village of Arts and Humanities, which then built more art parks, renovated homes, and created other programs. Lily Yeh trusted that her real purpose in life was unfolding, and in trusting, help came. Now her new organization, Barefoot Artists Inc., teaches residents and artists how to replicate her successful model in communities that have suffered around the world from Palestine and Rwanda to Syria and India.

When we trust that we are on track, and do what we love, we seem to be aligned with the flow of synchronicity. We ask for guidance and help and we seem to receive it. All around us the signs seem to confirm that we're doing the right thing for us. We have an expanded awareness of who we are and why we're here.

I trust that I'm heading in the right direction for my growth.

I am on track to fulfill my purpose.

3. Connecting with a power greater than ourselves

We may live in a secular society dominated by materialistic values and where religious institutions are largely discredited, but we also yearn for a deeper connection to something beyond our own egos. Falling in love, having a baby, or achieving something we set out to do that was challenging can give us a taste of joy, but as we all know, the feeling doesn't last. Although we're physical, emotional, mental, and social beings, we're also spiritual beings, we all have a Divine Spark within us, and for total wellbeing we need to be connected to the Source of life. Life has to have a spiritual dimension, as Caroline Myss, one of the leading writers in the field of consciousness and health, writes, "Again and again the sacred texts tell us that our life's purpose is to understand and develop the power of our spirit, power that is vital to our mental and physical wellbeing."

We're here to learn and grow and mature as human beings, reaching our full potential. Perhaps the soul in its wisdom chooses the conditions that will best help its growth in this lifetime. This is the idea that the Eastern religions call karma, the law of cause and effect, which means we cannot escape the consequences of our actions, either in this life or in past lives. Our souls at the moment of birth choose to work through karma, or postpone it until the next rebirth. Even if we find this concept difficult to accept, most of us have less difficulty with the idea of solely in this lifetime "reaping what we sowed," or "what goes around comes around," or "chickens coming home to roost." Our lives are very much a reflection of how we've spent them, as the writer Edith Wharton said so well, "People pay for what they do, and still more for what they have allowed themselves to become. And they pay for it simply: by the lives they lead."

The Latin root of the word religion is *religare*, meaning to reconnect. The purpose of religion was, and remains, to reconnect us to the Source of life. We can choose the path of growth, which is a spiritual journey, and which has been described in many ways. One of the oldest religions, Shinto, talks about

Finding our unique purpose
....
247

the divine way; for Buddhism it's the middle way; for Christianity it's the way of Christ; for Judaism it's the way of the Lord; and the Islamic term for religion in general is *mazhab*, meaning "the way." There may be many different ways, but at the heart of all the different traditions the essence is the same, to remember the Spark of Divinity that we have within us, and to reconnect with that power that is greater than ourselves so that we may fulfill our unique purpose.

I am a spiritual being.

I am connected to the Source of life.

I am reaching my full potential.

4. Following our own path—the heroine's journey

Many of us have succeeded in becoming strong and independent women in what is still, in many respects, a world in which men have most of the power. Although we may have done well on our outer journey through life, managing to keep all the balls in the air, we may well have paid a price in ending up feeling empty, exhausted, not good enough, or simply that we've been banging our heads against a brick wall, or climbing the wrong ladder.

This underlying sense of unease or alienation can, however, ultimately lead us to something deeper and richer. Often life has to fall apart before it can be transformed into something more fulfilling. It's when we're on our knees that we know we need to make the inner journey.

In every culture and at every time in history, in myths, epic poems, and novels, in fairy tales, films, and plays, the idea of the journey or quest, in which the hero or heroine leaves familiar surroundings, ventures forth, undergoes trials and tribulations, and eventually returns home wiser, or with the treasure or elixir, is a familiar pattern. It's also a template for how to look at our lives and the challenges we face when we want to discover who we really are and how we should live.

As women, we love to feel connected to others, in touch with our feminine nature, and able to express and be nourished by our creative capacities. If we've lived largely by masculine values and pursued a career, we may well have neglected these aspects of ourselves in our struggle to reach our goals. For women who have put their spouse's careers first and been subsumed with raising a family and homemaking, the opposite may be true, and they may want to

Finding our unique purpose

develop greater independence, strength, and courage to pursue something for themselves that they have not had the opportunity to explore before. We will all need to dive deep and bring to the surface the parts of ourselves we have not cultivated, and accept and integrate them, so that we can balance the masculine and feminine parts of ourselves.

When we choose to make the journey inward, we need time alone for quiet and reflection. We can ask for help and guidance, we can trust what we find, and as we discover greater clarity about what we need to do, we can make the necessary changes so that we achieve greater balance and can enjoy richer, more joyful lives.

I choose to make the journey inward.

I balance the masculine and feminine parts of myself.

I ask for help and guidance on my journey.

5. Harnessing the power of intention

Once we've chosen to live an authentic life in which we are in touch with our true selves and are clear about our purpose of doing what we love and through which we seek to find a way to help others, we need to set an intention. Intention is what wills something to happen, energized by the passion of the heart, or as the writer and spiritual teacher Gary Zukav puts it, it's "a quality of consciousness that infuses our action."

When we form an intention to do something, our brains not only direct our attention to what we can do now, but also to what we could do next. They help us pursue our goal with energy and enthusiasm, focusing our attention on what we can do, and looking for as many opportunities as possible. We become attuned throughout our whole being to achieving our goal, which is why intention is so powerful, and why we are more likely to achieve what we want to attain if we articulate it clearly.

The Universe seems to work with us when our intention is of the highest order and when we want the best both for ourselves and others. The help comes because we're following our hearts, and we're staying true to what we're passionate about, whilst at the same time feeling that we need to be of service. As things unfold, we can go with the flow, although we need to remember that there is a paradox with intention. We set our intention, but we have to surrender the outcome, letting the Universe take care of the process. Surrender is about being patient and

Finding our unique purpose
....

trusting, realizing and accepting that we're not in control.

🦋

I set my intention to _____ clearly.

I look for opportunities to serve others.

I go with the flow and surrender the outcome.

6. Making a difference through the work we do

Whatever we feel our unique purpose in life is, it's the wish to add value, to contribute, and to make a difference to other people's lives that makes our lives meaningful. We need meaning and are more personally motivated and involved and pursue our goals courageously and enthusiastically when life has meaning for us. It doesn't matter what it is that we do as our chosen work, but it's important that when we are working, we are working consciously and being the best we can be. The poet David Whyte writes: "Good work is work that makes sense and that grants sense and meaning to one who does it and to those affected by it."

We need to embrace our work and allow it to become our vocation, although that doesn't necessarily mean that it's the means by which we earn our money to pay the bills. Certainly there have been many who have had vocations that were different from their livelihood. Perhaps today things are changing: many more women now work for themselves than in the past, and are also reluctant to work just for a paycheck at the end of the month. We want to make a difference to people's lives through the work we do.

We want to use our gifts for the benefit of others. Kahlil Gibran, the Lebanese mystic and poet, described work as "love made visible." That's something worth striving for. In my own case, I love using my skill and knowledge and life experience to write books that I hope will inspire and help others. As a publisher of books previously, I also had the same sense of doing something meaningful that benefited others, even though this was also the means by which I made my living.

Just occasionally I've wondered whether it's self-indulgent on my part to sit in my beautiful attic reading, reflecting, and writing, and whether I should instead be out volunteering or campaigning, when there is so much that needs to be done, but deep down I know that this is what I love doing. That it is

Finding our unique purpose
....

of value to others I know from the letters and emails I have received. In terms of living an authentic life, I know that I'm more cut out for this work of solitude at this stage of my life. Rabindranath Tagore, one of my favorite poets, sums up this whole idea of service being the very thing that leads us to joy in these few lines:

> I slept and dreamt that life was joy
> I awoke and saw that life was service
> I acted and behold, service was joy.

I can make a difference through the work I do.

I can use my skills and talents to benefit others.

I am being the best I can be.

7. Recovering the soul

We know that survival is not the goal of life. It is being connected to the Source of life and to others. In other words, feeling whole instead of feeling split and separate. When we feel in harmony both within and without, joy can flow without being blocked.

Sometimes when we live our lives in survival mode, without the nourishment that connection gives us, we get ill, and we're forced to look at ourselves and how we're living. In indigenous cultures, illness is seen as a disturbance, as a split between body and soul, between the individual, family, and community, and the invisible realms, which is very different from how doctors look at a sick patient in western allopathic medicine. Healing by shamans and medicine women in traditional cultures is regarded as bringing all these elements back into balance. Illness is seen as a loss of soul, by which is meant a loss of purpose, meaning, and mystery. Healing for them is as much about recovering the soul as it is about restoring the body, and there are rituals and ceremonies to facilitate this.

Our modern medicine emphasizes cure, not healing, but if we choose to see meaning in illness, there can be the healing that our souls need. We have to overcome our confusion, anger, and grief at what has happened to us. Through the suffering we experience when ill, we are challenged to think about what is important to us, to reconsider our values, to take responsibility, and to make different choices about how we live our lives. We listen to feelings and promptings more, and we live in new ways that are

Finding our unique purpose

more aware. Meditation, yoga, chanting, prayer, and ritual help us stay connected to the Source.

Suffering opens us up, expands us, and helps us understand who we really are. We find strength and courage, and a greater capacity for compassion for others. We change our perception of how things are, and free ourselves from old patterns of thinking and feeling, so that a different kind of future is possible.

I recognize that I am part of the whole.

I choose harmony within and without.

I live in balance.

8. Enhancing our lives now

So often we put off living today. We're so busy keeping up appearances, working for our paycheck, rushing around trying to keep the show on the road if we have a family, cramming everything in, keeping up with our emails, organizing our diaries, rather than doing what we most love to do. Next month when I've finished that assignment, we say, or next year, when I've made enough money, or the year after next when the children have started university, I'll have a bit more time . . . We behave as if we have forever, though underneath it all, if we stop to ask ourselves, we may well be afraid of contracting a serious illness, or having an accident, or being caught up in a terrorist attack.

Cardinal Newman famously warned us: "Fear not that thy life shall come to an end, but rather fear that it shall never have a beginning."

We cannot put off doing what we long to do and living authentically. We owe it to ourselves to have the most fulfilling and rewarding life we can possibly have, and we can start right now. As Elizabeth Kübler-Ross, the pioneering psychiatrist who wrote on death and dying, reminds us:

> It is not the end of the physical body that should worry us. Rather our concern must be to live while we're alive—to release our inner selves from the spiritual death that comes with living behind a façade designed to conform to external definitions of who and what we are. Every individual human being born on this earth has the capacity to become a unique and special person unlike any who has ever existed before or will ever exist again.

When we realize our uniqueness, and have faith in ourselves and pursue our purpose with passion, we have a zest for life and radiate joy.

I realize my uniqueness.
Now is the time for me to live authentically.
I pursue my purpose with passion.

9. Linking our purpose with that of the whole

We live in extraordinary times of escalating and complex change, which means we face both danger and opportunity. On every front we seem to be faced with crises—environmental, social, economic, and political. These crises are largely the result of our limited consciousness and our attitudes and behaviors. We know that attitudes and behaviors can be changed if the intention is there. We can start where we are, see things as they are, and consciously choose to change. "Change yourself and you have done your part in changing the world," wrote Paramahansa Yogananda, the inspirational Indian teacher who introduced so many of us Westerners to meditation through his classic *Autobiography of a Yogi*.

We have to start with ourselves, and when we open our hearts and feel empathy for our fellow human beings, we can make a difference. And we are not alone. Our individual purpose is linked with the whole through our intentions, thoughts, and actions. We are each part of the energy field, and our purpose is to work in harmony with all living beings. The opportunities for service and creative participation are available to us all.

Just as crises in our own lives are wakeup calls, forcing change and realignment with the Source of life, so may we be looking at a collective wakeup call for the whole planet, demanding major cultural change and reorientation to more spiritual, life-enhancing values. Barbara Marx Hubbard, the futurist who has been at the forefront of the movement for conscious evolution, writes:

> We feel many millions of us, within our cells a rising intuition, a yearning to be more, to create more, to participate more, to help more in the healing and evolving of a suffering world. And that spiritual impulse . . . is the impulse of Evolution, awakening in us—whatever our religion, whatever our faith, whatever our culture—transcending all of the past.

Finding our unique purpose

Like the oft-used comparison of the butterfly emerging from the chrysalis, we are waking up both individually and collectively to a new life and a better world. We are choosing to create a future that is fairer, more cooperative, more sustainable, and capable of greater progress for everyone, both now and for future generations. This is our unique purpose— we are meant to be here and part of the unfolding mystery of human evolution.

My unique purpose is linked with that of the whole.

I commit to playing my part in creating a better future for all.

I choose joy.

You are

You are wiser than you know, more courageous than
   you guess.
You are stronger than you feel in the greatness of
   your soul.
You are younger than your years; you are beautiful
   to see.
You can hold your joy complete underneath emotion's
   tears.
You are loved beyond your dreams, far more special
   than you think.
You are one with the Divine. Life is kinder than it
   seems.
Child of God, accept that love caring, singing
   through your mind.
Every miracle is yours. You are wonderful. Believe!

MARGERY JOHNSON

About the Author

Photo by Bill McCosh

Eileen Campbell is a writer of inspirational books, including a successful series of anthologies described by the media as "treasures of timeless wisdom," which sold collectively around 250,000 copies. She has studied with a variety of teachers from different traditions and brings a wealth of knowledge and life experience to her books. She is known for her pioneering and visionary career as a self-help and spirituality publisher, and has also written and presented for BBC Radio 2 and 4. She currently devotes her energies to yoga, writing, and gardening. She lives in England.